Edited by
S. W. BURTON
H. S. AKISKAL

Dysthymic Disorder

GASKELL

ISBN 0 902241 33 8

Gaskell is an imprint of the Royal College of Psychiatrists,
17 Belgrave Square, London SW1

Distributed in North America
by American Psychiatric Press, Inc.
ISBN 0 88048 600 7

A CIP catalogue record for this book is
available from the British Library.

Typeset by Dobbie Typesetting Limited, Plymouth, Devon
Printed in Great Britain

It is with great sadness that I have to relate that some months after kindly submitting the Foreword, Professor Max Hamilton died.

His contribution on the day of the symposium which forms the basis for this book was considerable and lively. Professor Hamilton taught several generations of psychiatrists in Leeds and I am glad to say I was among them. His great intellect illuminated the rather gloomy subject of statistics for me early on in my medical studies and later he presented a sharp and penetrating analysis of clinical psychopathology.

He will be missed.

SWB

I first met Dr Burton in September, 1986, in the Michelangelo Hotel, Milan, Italy, where I was participating in a psychiatric conference, and he had flown from London to discuss with me the idea of a symposium on the newly introduced DSM–III concept of dysthymia. We met in that particular hotel by chance, but I nevertheless find it noteworthy because, in a letter written to his father in 1512, Michelangelo had written: "I lead a miserable existence . . . I live wearied by stupendous labours and beset by a thousand anxieties. And thus I have lived for some fifteen years now and never an hour's happiness have I had." A symposium devoted to the nature of such protracted dysphoric states, which burden the sufferer not so much because of their intensity, but more so because of their duration, is the challenge that Dr Burton wanted us to undertake.

I was ambivalent at first: what could DSM–III mean to European psychiatrists — especially the sceptical British? My ambivalence melted away, however, as I observed the enthusiasm with which Dr Burton argued how a trans-Atlantic dialogue would serve the cause of greater recognition of the affective origin of some of these protracted emotional states that were categorised as character disorders. I had always frowned upon the practice of diagnosing character disorder before a fair therapeutic trial with thymoleptic agents and, therefore, Dr Burton's plea fell on receptive ears. The rest is history as recorded in this book.

I thoroughly enjoyed the encounter with distinguished colleagues in London. I am particularly honoured that the dialogue with Professor Max Hamilton continued, through correspondence and other international meetings, until his death. After his retirement from the Chair at the University of Leeds, Professor Hamilton continued treating very ill patients and, till the end, was eager to learn everything he could about the treatment of chronic-resistant depressives. Although we are all saddened by his departure, in a sense he is still very much with us because of all that he taught us about depression and patients.

HSA

Contents

List of contributors

Professor H. S. Akiskal, Professor of Psychiatry and Pharmacology, and Director of Section of Affective Disorders, University of Tennessee, Memphis, Department of Psychiatry, 66N Pauline St, Suite 633, Memphis, TN 38163, USA

Dr G. T. Bell, Senior Lecturer and Honorary Consultant in Psychiatry, Medical College of St Bartholomew's Hospital, West Smithfield, London EC1A 7BE

Dr K. W. Bridges, Consultant Psychiatrist, Department of Psychiatry, The Manchester Royal Infirmary, Oxford Road, Manchester M13 9BX

Dr S. W. Burton, Locum Consultant Psychiatrist, The Gordon Hospital, Bloomburg Street, London SW1

Professor G. B. Cassano, Professor of Psychiatry, Institute of Clinical Psychiatry, University of Pisa, Via Roma 67, 56100, Pisa, Italy

Dr S. A. Checkley, Consultant Psychiatrist, Maudsley Hospital, Denmark Hill, London SE5 8AZ

Dr J. F. W. Deakin, Senior Lecturer in Psychiatry, University of Manchester, Department of Psychiatry, The University Hospital of South Manchester, West Didsbury, Manchester M20 8LR

Professor D. P. Goldberg, Mental Illness Research Unit, University of Manchester, The University Hospital of South Manchester, West Didsbury, Manchester M20 8LR

Dr R. M. A. Hirschfeld, Chief, Mood, Anxiety, and Personality Disorders Research Branch, National Institute of Mental Health, Parklawn Building, Room 10C–24, 5600 Fishers Lane, Rockville, MD 20857, USA

Dr C. L. E. Katona, Senior Lecturer and Honorary Consultant in Psychiatry, University College and Middlesex School of Medicine, Middlesex Hospital, London W1N 8AA

Dr M. B. Keller, Director, Outpatient Research, Massachusetts General Hospital, Associate Professor Harvard Medical School, c/o Lindemann Mental Health Center, 25 Staniford Street, Room 517, Boston, MA 02114, USA

Dr I. Maremmani, Institute of Clinical Psychiatry, University of Pisa, Italy
Dr D. Murphy, Senior Registrar, Maudsley Hospital, Denmark Hill, London SE5 8AZ
Dr G. Perugi, Institute of Clinical Psychiatry, University of Pisa, Italy
Dr Z. Rihmer, Psychiatrist and Neurologist, Director and Head, In- and Outpatient Department of Psychiatry, No. XIII, National Institute for Nervous and Mental Diseases, Orszagos Ideg- es Eimegyogyaszati Intezet, Budapest II, Voroshadsereg u. 116, Hungary
Dr N. Seivewright, Consultant in Drug Dependence, Regional Drugs Dependence Service, Prestwich Hospital, Bury New Road, Prestwich, Manchester M25 7BL, formerly Research Fellow and Honorary Senior Registrar, Mapperley Hospital, Nottingham
Ms F. M. Sessa, Research Analyst, Massachusetts General Hospital, Boston, Massachusetts, USA
Dr P. Tyrer, Senior Lecturer in Psychiatry, St Charles' Hospital, Exmoor Street, London W10 6DZ, formerly Consultant Psychiatrist, Mapperley Hospital, Nottingham

Foreword

MAX HAMILTON

DSM–III is the psychiatric classification system which is criticised by everybody. Yet it is a great advance on DSM–II and could well be described as a revolutionary advance. One of its most controversial categories is that of dysthymic disorder.

Dysthymia lies on the border between the normal and the pathological. It is fundamental in clinical psychiatry that one should distinguish between normal depression, which is a distressed state occurring as a reaction to loss, and abnormal depression, which is a changed and abnormal state of the individual. It is not sufficient to describe the former as a mood and the latter as a disorder. The really important distinction is between an appropriate reaction (given the nature of human beings) to a serious change in the circumstances of an individual and a changed pattern of behaviour which is independent of those circumstances.

The great difficulty is that the abnormal reaction can be precipitated by an appropriate stress. If it is severe, it is not too difficult to recognise it as a disorder, but when it is mild, and especially when it is long standing, the clinician is faced with great difficulties in making a diagnosis and prescribing appropriate treatment.

The symposium recorded in this book was one of the first, if not the first, to be devoted to this subject. Among the speakers were representatives of all opinions, from those who regard dysthymia as being little or nothing more than a reaction to continuous stress, to those who recognise it as being the mild form of depressive illness, whether unipolar or bipolar, requiring little more than the standard treatments for affective illness.

Of course, the symposiasts recognised that the one name covers a great variety of conditions. These include the depressive variety of prodromal phases of depressive illness, very mild depressive states, incomplete recovery from acute illness, reaction to long-standing social and personal problems and, very likely, a particular type of personality. An important problem is that concerning the relationship between dysthymia and anxiety states.

Under one name or another, and usually several, dysthymia has always been with us. Did not Shakespeare give us an immortal delineation in the "melancholy Jacques"? The fact that this book has been written is an indication of an important change in the outlook of psychiatrists. It has been a platitude of textbooks that mental illness develops from an interaction of (stressful) circumstances with a constitutional predisposition. Until comparatively recently, the main interest of psychiatrists was in the circumstances that precipitated mental illness. This was where one could apply the 'therapeutic lever' through social therapy and psychotherapy. The steady progress and development of biological methods of treatment have directed attention to the constitutional basis of mental illness. Its importance has been emphasised by genetic and twin studies and, above all, by adoption studies.

At one time, those who investigated the constitutional basis of mental illness were regarded as accepting an attitude of therapeutic nihilism. This was certainly untrue in internal medicine, as exemplified by the specialty of endocrine disease. Modern biochemical, pharmacological and genetic research is rapidly demonstrating that this applies equally to psychiatry. This book deals not only with the advance in knowledge and understanding, and the recognition of our still great ignorance, but also makes clear that psychiatrists still recognise that sick people need comfort, help, and reassurance in addition to scientifically based skilled treatment.

Max Hamilton

Emeritus Professor
Leeds
England

Introduction

S. W. BURTON

Dysthymic disorder, or dysthymia, was defined for the first time in a systematic way in the American DSM–III in 1980, in an attempt to collate a spectrum of chronic mild depressive disorders under a single heading for diagnostic and research purposes. Research experience with the resulting classification has until recently been confined to North America, but with the spread of influence of DSM–III, its successor DSM–III–R, and ICD-10 (which also includes a category called 'dysthymia'), studies in Europe have begun to explore its utility as a diagnostic concept.

Subacute or chronic subclinical depression may be much more common than has been thought hitherto, and is probably inextricably merged with disordered personality, yet the first challenge for medical as opposed to social interventions must be correct diagnosis thus enabling the application of appropriate treatments. Research experience of dysthymia from North America and elsewhere should be of interest to those psychiatrists and primary care physicians who routinely treat patients whose symptoms and history fall short of establishing a diagnosis of major depressive disorder.

This book reflects a wide range of experience of the use of the diagnostic category of dysthymia from the theoretical to the clinically pragmatic. The chapters represent papers given at a special meeting of the Biological Group of the Royal College of Psychiatrists, held at the Royal Society of Medicine in London. The meeting, entitled 'Dysthymic Disorder: A New Concept in Chronic Mild Depression', took place on a hot day in June 1987, which, coincidentally, also saw voters going to the polls in a British General Election.

On behalf of all those who attended the meeting I wish to express our considerable gratitude to the Janssen Research Foundation whose generous support made the meeting possible.

My personal thanks are also due both to Gerry Hammond at Janssen and Mrs Cheryl Brinsden who has patiently typed (and retyped) the manuscripts before and after editing.

1 Towards a definition of dysthymia: boundaries with personality and mood disorders

H. S. AKISKAL

Systematic clinical observations, family history, and laboratory findings have led to the reclassification of many patients, formerly diagnosed as having personality and neurotic disorders, into clinically meaningful subtypes of chronic depression, many of which have been shown to respond to thymoleptic drugs. The new diagnostic rubric of 'dysthymic disorder' has been introduced into the official classification of the American Psychiatric Association (in DSM–III, 1980) to encompass this heterogeneous realm of mixed characterological and low-grade affective pathology.

This change, which for some represents a radical departure from traditional nosology, was in part based on prospective follow-up of neurotic depressives which demonstrated a recurrent (endogenous) unipolar or bipolar outcome in as many as 40% of cases (Akiskal *et al*, 1978). This and related considerations (Klerman *et al*, 1979) necessitated reclassifying many neurotic depressions into the general category of mood disorders. There was a consequent need to create the rubric of 'dysthymia', also subsumed under mood disorders, for the remaining cases of neurotic depression that pursued a low-grade intermittent or chronic course (Akiskal, 1983*a*). These changes represent more than a terminological revision; they counter a widespread clinical stereotype that equates protracted depressions with character pathology.

The thesis of this chapter is that psychopharmacological advances will eventually shrink the universe of so-called 'character' disorders. It is not my goal here to discuss in detail all possible clinical pathways to chronic dysphoria: for instance, the contribution of cyclothymic and rapid-cycling mood disorders to what in North America is labelled 'borderline personality' (Akiskal *et al*, 1985) is beyond the scope of this chapter. My main intention here is to highlight ways in which careful subtyping of chronic depressions can enhance clinical practice. Towards that end, I review research findings from the University of Tennessee in the context of other developments on both sides of the Atlantic. Following a brief discussion about inadequacy of treatment as a factor in the chronicity of depression, I explore the boundaries of dysthymia with personality and primary mood disorders. Its boundary with anxiety disorders, which represents an even greater challenge (Akiskal & Lemmi, 1987), is discussed in Chapters 3 and 9. As the material of the present chapter integrates previous research reports (Akiskal *et al*, 1980, 1981, 1984; Rosenthal *et al*, 1981; Akiskal, 1982) and clinical descriptive papers (Akiskal, 1983*a*, 1984; Akiskal & Haykal, 1988), the reader is referred to these sources for further details on methodological and psychopathological aspects.

Chronicity and treatment failure

Any discussion of chronic depression must first address the adequacy of treatment. Despite major therapeutic advances, recent data (Keller *et al*, 1982) indicate that two out of three depressed patients, including many seen in psychiatric settings, do not receive adequate treatment. Such treatment failure represents a complex interaction between factors that pertain to pharmacology, the patient, and the physician (Akiskal, 1985). Pharmacological factors ultimately translate into inadequate dosage or duration of tricyclic antidepressant (TCA) trials, and only rarely to low TCA blood level despite adequate dose. Patient factors that can undermine therapy include a mistaken fear of dependence or addiction, hypochondriacal concerns about side-effects and, sometimes, outright rejection of any pharmacological interventions for what they view as personal or 'moral' problems. Certain attitudes of physicians may also lead to treatment failure secondary to underuse of effective treatments. Those with psychotherapeutic orientation—often ambivalent about using medication for a 'psychological' disorder—may place undue emphasis on the characterological aspects of the illness, paying minimal attention to the symptomatic picture of the illness; others tend to rely heavily on TCAs, sometimes to the exclusion of monoamine oxidase inhibitors (MAOIs) or electroconvulsive therapy (ECT).

Thus, multiple factors underlie treatment failure in what is the most treatable of all psychiatric disorders. Many affectively ill patients, at least in North America, are prematurely declared 'treatment-resistant', a label which robs them of appropriate thymoleptic treatments. However, inadequate treatment cannot be equated with chronic depression; many depressed individuals present in clinical settings with established chronicity predating any treatment efforts. This is particularly true for many dysthymic patients.

The tendency to equate 'chronicity' with 'character pathology' further compromises the proper recognition of the affective pathology in chronically depressed patients (Price, 1978). At best, and again this reflects North American practice, these patients are considered 'atypical depressives' and, at worst, as 'borderlines'. These labels, especially the latter, often reflect the frustration clinicians experience in their attempts to treat the unfathomable moods of these very difficult patients (Akiskal *et al*, 1985).

Subsuming these patients under the term 'neurotic depression' is also problematic, because of the implication that response to pharmacotherapy would be unsatisfactory. The increasing availability of newer pharmacological approaches to depression is one of the reasons for the broadening of the North American concept of affective illness that includes chronicity, now sanctioned in the official American nosology within the DSM–III category of 'dysthymic disorder' (American Psychiatric Association, 1980).

DSM–III and DSM–III–R concepts of dysthymia

Dysthymic disorder in DSM–III subsumed all chronic depressions of two or more years. In the latest revision, in DSM–III–R (American Psychiatric Association, 1987), low-grade depressive states following major depressive episodes, now classified as major depression with partial remission, are distinguished from dysthymia proper, a disorder of insidious onset, low-grade severity and a chronic course. Dysthymia can also be categorised as either 'secondary'—if it develops in the setting of another major psychiatric disorder—or 'primary'. The dysthymic category in DSM–III–R refers to this primary subtype with insidious origin, which is often in childhood or adolescence. Its key characteristics are:

(a) low-grade chronicity (>2 years) which is not residual of a major depression
(b) insidious onset with origin often in childhood or adolescence
(c) persistent or intermittent course
(d) concurrent 'character' pathology
(e) ambulatory disorder compatible with 'stable' social functioning.

Two points should be emphasised. Chronicity does not imply presence of symptoms on a daily basis; intermittent symptoms are quite common. Indeed, Angst & Dobler-Mikola (1985) have described brief recurrent depressions which are as prevalent as major depressions and which, conceivably, form a 'bridge' between dysthymia and major mood disorders. Secondly, it is noteworthy that in DSM–III–R personality disorder is considered to be present *concurrently* with dysthymia. This is an important change from DSM–III which, despite its philosophy of considering personality disorders (Axis II) as orthogonal to the major psychiatric syndromes (Axis I), contained the ambiguous statement that "often the affective features of [dysthymia] are viewed as secondary to an underlying personality disorder."

All of the foregoing revisions in DSM–III–R led to a much more circumscribed concept of dysthymia than that in DSM–III. There is, nevertheless, some disagreement in the literature (see, for instance, Kocsis & Frances,

1987) over whether such a core dysthymic group can be distinguished from other depressive disorders. For this reason, it would be first instructive to examine the characteristics of major depressions with incomplete recovery.

Major depression with partial remission

The course of primary depressive illness with late onset (after 40 years) can be quite protracted (Akiskal, 1982). Although the pre-morbid history may be free of depressive manifestations, residual depressive symptoms are common, and chronicity may develop after one or several depressive episodes that fail to remit fully. During this residual phase (Cassano *et al*, 1983), which may linger on for months, or even years, 'characterological' manifestations (a sense of resignation, inhibited communication, rigidity, irritability or emotional lability) may dominate the clinical picture. The lives of these people are often characterised by overdedication to work and inability to enjoy leisure activities (DeLisio *et al*, 1986). Marital conflict is often in a state of chronic deadlock, with patients unable to divorce or to reconcile with spouses (Akiskal *et al*, 1981). In other patients, the residual state is dominated by somatic manifestations involving vegetative or autonomic nervous system irregularities (Weissman & Klerman, 1977).

In comparing chronic with acute depressives in a study at the University of Tennessee (Akiskal, 1982), shortened REM latency was demonstrated in both groups of in-patients. This neurophysiological similarity suggested the value of conceptualising the chronic phase as an affective process. This conclusion was further buttressed by familial affective loading in the chronic group. Psychosocial and biological stressors also appeared relevant to chronic outcome: chronic depressives were significantly more likely to have disabled spouses, multiple losses of immediate family members through death, concurrent disabling medical illness, use of catecholamine-depleting antihypertensive agents, and history of excessive use of alcohol and sedative hypnotic agents. Failure to recover from acute depressive episodes would thus appear to be based on multiple factors. The Newcastle chronic depression study (Scott *et al*, 1988) has supported many of the Tennessee findings.

After removal of contributory pharmacological factors (e.g. reserpine, benzodiazepines, or alcohol), most patients with chronic residual depressions can be satisfactorily managed by vigorous chemotherapy (Ward *et al*, 1979; Ayd, 1984). The physician can begin the treatment regime with one of the classic TCAs in combination with supportive psychotherapy and interpersonal psychotherapy (Weissman & Akiskal, 1984). Non-responsive patients can be given a full trial of a dissimilar TCA, or one of the newer antidepressants such as fluoxetine. Other patients may require ECT. Only a minority of patients prove to be refractory to these therapeutic interventions (Akiskal, 1985); occult malignancies, endocrine abnormalities, or neurological diseases are not uncommonly discovered. These considerations pertain primarily to unipolar depressives. The protracted mixed states that complicate the course of depressions superimposed on cyclothymic or hyperthymic temperaments require different strategies which involve, among others, lithium, thyroid hormone, and carbamazepine (Akiskal & Mallya, 1987). Although these protracted mixed states mimic dysthymia, they represent a special type of residual state, and are not further discussed here.

Early-onset primary dysthymia

Dysthymia, literally 'ill-humoured', refers to individuals with the disposition to low-grade dysphoria. The classic picture of dysthymia is that of an individual who is habitually gloomy, brooding, overconscientious, incapable of fun, and preoccupied with personal inadequacy (Akiskal, 1983*a*). As discussed earlier, insidious onset of dysphoria, dating back to late childhood or teens, preceding any superimposed major depressive episodes by years, or even decades, represents the most typical developmental background of dysthymia in DSM–III–R. Return to the low-grade depressive pattern is the rule following recovery from superimposed episodes, if any; hence the designation 'double depression' (Keller *et al*, 1983). Dysthymic patients often complain of being depressed 'since conception' or of 'feeling miserable all the time'. They also seem to view themselves as belonging to 'an aristocracy of suffering' (Schneider, 1958). These descriptions of chronic dysphoria in the absence of observed signs of melancholia often earn patients the label of 'characterological depression' (Akiskal *et al*, 1980). The difficulty of separating the fluctuating course of depression from the patient's character structure is often reflected in diagnostic uncertainties and therapeutic impasse.

Such difficulty notwithstanding, it has been possible to delineate the symptom profile of these patients with sufficient precision (McCullough, 1988). The core clinical manifestations of dysthymia are:

(a) mood
- (i) anhedonia
- (ii) depression

(b) vegetative
- (i) insomnia
- (ii) hypersomnia

(c) cognitive
- (i) low self-esteem
- (ii) guilty ruminations
- (iii) hopelessness
- (iv) suicidal ideation

(d) psychomotor
  (i) poor concentration
  (ii) fatigue
  (iii) reduced interests
  (iv) social withdrawal

This list obviously overlaps with that of major depression, but differs from it in that symptoms outnumber signs (more 'subjective' than 'objective' depression). Thus, marked disturbances in appetite and libido are uncharacteristic and severe psychomotor agitation or retardation are absent. All of this translates into a depression which is less intense in its symptomatic picture. A related feature of dysthymia which sets it apart from major depression is that it is not sharply demarcated from the sufferer's usual self. In our view, if the change from 'dysthymia' to 'major depression' occurs gradually, which is often the case, dysthymia should still be considered the basic disorder; only a precipitous fall into depression would qualify for a major depressive diagnosis. In other words, 'double depressions' (see Chapter 2), are more like dysthymia than episodic major depression. The recent findings of Klein *et al* (1988) tend to support this position.

Utilising the strategy of pharmacological dissection, championed by Klein *et al* (1980), we undertook a systematic study of early-onset low-grade depressives (Akiskal *et al*, 1980). Our findings led to the suggestion that these patients could be divided into predominantly affective (subaffective dysthymic) and characterological (character spectrum) groups based on response to a rigorous pharmacological trial (at least two secondary amine TCAs, and/or lithium carbonate) given in the context of 'practical psychotherapy'. This psychotherapeutic approach is described in our original report (Akiskal, 1980). Differences in clinical features, family history, REM latency, and course supported the tentative distinction made on the basis of treatment response.

Subaffective dysthymia

Patients in this subgroup had the shortened REM latencies (less than 70 minutes on consecutive nights), characteristic of acute primary major depressions, and showed favourable response to TCAs, lithium, or both. Similarity to primary affective disorder was confirmed by the presence of anhedonic, guilt-ridden, or hypersomnic retarded features. Family history was positive for both unipolar and bipolar affective disorder. The personality of these patients conformed to Schneider's depressive typology as operationalised at the University of Tennessee. Based on this and more recent research findings (reviewed by Akiskal, 1989), we have revised these criteria for a categorical identification of a depressive temperament:

(a) introverted, passive, or lethargic
(b) gloomy, humourless, or incapable of fun
(c) given to worry, brooding, or pessimism
(d) preoccupied with inadequacy, failure and negative events
(e) self-critical, self-reproachful and prone to guilt
(f) sceptical, overcritical, or complaining

The term 'temperament', as opposed to 'personality', underscores its close link to the underlying affective biology.

Taken together, these findings suggest that thymoleptic-responsive, early-onset dysthymia is best viewed as a milder, lifelong expression of primary affective disorder—hence, the adjective 'subaffective' to qualify this subtype of dysthymia. However, while these patients pursued a predominantly 'unipolar' course, they also displayed subtle bipolar tendencies such as brief hypomanic switches on TCA challenge. Kovacs & Gastsonis (1989), in their prospective follow-up of dysthymic children, also found that many developed hypomania. As proposed elsewhere (Akiskal, 1983*b*), some dysthymic conditions are on a nosological continuum with cyclothymic and hyperthymic (chronic hypomanic) disorders. This suggestion is based on the following shared characteristics: bipolar familial history similar to classic bipolar controls; and the occurrence of hypomania, either spontaneously (cyclothymic and hyperthymic groups), or pharmacologically mobilised (dysthymic and cyclothymic groups). Thus, dysthymia, as defined here, emerges as a less penetrant disorder in the spectrum of cycloid affective temperaments (Kretschmer, 1936). In the ambulatory setting of the University of Tennessee mood clinic, which receives referrals of many 'resistant' patients, such a subaffective group accounted for 10–15% of a broadly defined 'chronic depressive' population. This proportion is probably much higher in the unselected psychiatric private and general medical practice settings where it may account for 50–60% of chronically dysphoric patients. I base this figure on the impressive response rate in the Kocsis *et al* (1988) double-blind controlled study of imipramine in dysthymics at the Cornell Payne-Whitney Clinic, which is a private facility.*

Character spectrum disorder

This designation reflects a *mélange* of dependent, histrionic, and antisocial traits. Patients in this subgroup, who constituted two-thirds of the

*Presenting the various psychotherapeutic strategies for dysthymic patients is beyond the scope of this chapter. As discussed elsewhere (Weissman & Akiskal, 1984; Akiskal & Haykal, 1988), these should include helping the patients to capitalise on positive changes in the environment and steering them to environments (e.g. jobs and object choices) best suited for their temperaments. As these individuals tend to be dependent on and dependable in their work, proper vocational guidance is very important. Kretschmer's ideas on the cycloid-depressive temperaments (1936) can provide further insights into this aspect of the management of dysthymics.

early-onset chronic dysphorics in the Tennessee study, failed to show appreciable response to our systematic clinical trials. Their REM latencies were in the normal range (70–110 minutes). Superimposed syndromal depressive episodes, if any, lacked melancholic features. Other characteristics included polydrug and alcohol abuse, high rates of familial alcoholism, and parental assortative mating (i.e. both parents ill with alcoholism and personality disorder but no affective illness). These findings indicate an absence of external validating criteria for affective illness and suggest that this lifelong disorder is best characterised as a dysphoric condition developing in the context of an early unstable familial environment and representing a variant of histrionic-antisocial personality. This disorder overlaps considerably with Winokur's (1979) 'depression spectrum disease', an early-onset disorder with tempestuous life history and superimposed depressive conditions occurring in the offspring of adult alcoholic or sociopathic probands. Our preference for their characterisation as 'character spectrum' stems from the prominence of lifelong personality disturbances (VanValkenburg *et al*, 1987) in the absence of external validating criteria for mood disorders.

Although, by definition, desipramine, nortriptyline and/or lithium were found to be ineffective in those dysthymic patients we considered to suffer from a 'character spectrum disorder', a subset may represent residual or adult attention deficit disorder (Wood *et al*, 1976) and could, potentially, benefit from low-dose stimulants or imipramine given in the context of a psycho-educational approach. Furthermore, MAOIs may be useful for those with clinical features approximating the rare syndrome of 'hysteroid dysphoria' (Liebowitz & Klein, 1979; Liebowitz *et al*, 1988). Finally, the experimental agent ritanserin has shown promising results in several European trials (Reyntjens *et al*, 1986; Murphy & Checkley, 1988; Bersani *et al*, 1988; Meco *et al*, 1988). It is also our clinical impression that other serotonergic antidepressants such as fluoxetine might be particularly well suited for dysthymic patients. These considerations underlie the optimistic thesis of this chapter, namely, that the advent of newer psycho-pharmacological agents could, ultimately, justify the reclassification of many dysphoric 'characterologically' disturbed patients into clinically dysthymic subtypes.

To date, three other groups of investigators have attempted to validate the distinction between subaffective dysthymia and character spectrum disorder based on external validating strategies similar to those of the Tennessee studies. Hauri & Sateia (1984) have replicated our sleep EEG findings. The more clinical studies by Rihmer and associates in Budapest (see Chapter 10) have revealed major differences in response to dexa-methasone suppression, thymoleptic agents, and sleep deprivation as predicted by the proposed distinction. Finally, Klein *et al* (1988) have identified one subgroup of dysthymics with endogenous depressive features, Schneiderian personality traits, bipolar family history and who may, during prospective follow-up, develop hypomania; and another subgroup with lifelong characterological instability and substance abuse.

Concluding remarks

Despite considerable overlap between dysthymic, neurotic and primary characterological pathology, I have attempted to summarise the heuristic value of the concept of dysthymia conceived as a variant of mood disorder. More specifically, I have proposed to limit the operational territory of dysthymia to a core early-onset subaffective category.

The difficulty in separating the habitual self of the patient from low-grade depression has led some to question if, for instance, the depressive personality in the Schneiderian sense is different from dysthymia conceived as a subaffective disorder (Hirschfeld *et al*, 1989). As I see it, they are in a continuum, dysthymia representing the more symptomatic (more 'sick') expression of a disposition to depressive illness. It should be borne in mind, however, that not all dysthymia, not even early-onset primary dysthymia, arises from a depressive temperamental substrate; for instance, the character spectrum group, which would meet the symptomatic criteria for dysthymia, is more histrionic-antisocial in personality structure. The depressive temperament as defined in this chapter can also be one of the possible precursors of major depressive, and even bipolar, disorders (Cassano *et al*, 1988), though prospective validation on this point is still lacking.

The rationale for the re-conceptualisation of at least some dysthymias as variants of mood disorder can now be defended by external validation strategies such as course, family history, biological markers and pharmacological dissection. North American clinicians have responded with greater enthusiasm in the utilisation of pharmacological interventions in low-grade depressions. The beneficial effects of pharmacotherapy are not limited to symptomatic improvement, but often involve substantial amelioration of interpersonal and social functions (Kocsis *et al*, 1988; Stewart *et al*, 1988). The resultant enthusiasm has led to therapeutic trials with both cyclic antidepressants and MAOIs. Given what we know about the clinical features, the sleep physiology, and the protracted nature of dysthymic conditions that interface with personality disorders, new thymoleptic agents that work on the serotonin system might prove even more rewarding.

It is also noteworthy that even psychoanalytically orientated psychiatrists now tend to endorse the view that in special subgroups of dysthymic patients the character pathology could represent defences to an underlying affective dysregulation (Cooper, 1986):

> "There is a group of chronically depressed and anxious patients . . . whose mood regulation is vastly changed by antidepressant medication. The entry of these new molecules into their metabolism alters, tending

to normalize the way they see the world, the way they do battle with their superegos, the way they respond to object separation. It may be that we have been co-conspirators with these patients in their need to construct a rational-seeming world in which they hold themselves unconsciously responsible for events. Narcissistic needs may lead these patients to claim control over uncontrollable behaviours rather than to admit to the utter helplessness of being at the mercy of mood that sweeps over them without apparent rhyme or reasons. An attempt at dynamic understanding in these situations may not only be genuinely explanatory, it may be a cruel misunderstanding of the patient's efforts to rationalize his life experience and may result in strengthening masochistic defenses.''

Much work lies ahead of us. But clinicians—who must often treat the difficult group of dysthymic patients before definite evidence of the effectiveness of specific psychopharmacological agents for this indication—have an important role to play in such progress. By the same token, they are also in the best position to judge the utility, or lack of utility, of the concept of dysthymia.

References

AKISKAL, H. S. (1982) Factors associated with incomplete recovery in primary depressive illness. *Journal of Clinical Psychiatry*, **43**, 266–271.

—— (1983*a*) Dysthymic disorder: psychopathology of proposed chronic depressive subtypes. *American Journal of Psychiatry*, **140**, 11–20.

—— (1983*b*) The bipolar spectrum: new concepts in classification and diagnosis. In *Psychiatry 1983: The American Psychiatric Association Annual Review* (ed. L. Grinspoon). Washington, DC: American Psychiatric Association.

—— (1984) Interface of chronic depression with personality and anxiety disorders. *Psychopharmacology Bulletin*, **20**, 393–398.

—— (1985) A proposed clinical approach to clinical and ''resistant'' depressions: evaluation and treatment. *Journal of Clinical Psychiatry*, **46**, 31–36.

—— (1989) Validating affective personality types. In *The Validity of Psychiatric Diagnosis* (ed. L. Robins), pp. 217–227. New York: Raven Press.

——, BITAR, A. H., PUZANTIAN, V. R., *et al* (1978) The nosological status of neurotic depression: a prospective three-to-four year examination in light of the primary-secondary and unipolar-bipolar dichotomies. *Archives of General Psychiatry*, **35**, 756–766.

——, ROSENTHAL, T. L., HAYKAL, R. F., *et al* (1980) Characterological depressions: clinical and sleep EEG findings separating ''subaffective dysthymias'' from ''character-spectrum'' disorders. *Archives of General Psychiatry*, **37**, 777–783.

——, KING, D., ROSENTHAL, T. L., *et al* (1981) Chronic depressions: Part 1. Clinical and familial characteristics in 137 probands. *Journal of Affective Disorders*, **3**, 297–311.

——, LEMMI, H., DICKSON, H., *et al* (1984) Chronic depressions: Part 2. Sleep EEG differentiation of primary dysthymic disorders from anxious depressions. *Journal of Affective Disorders*, **6**, 287–295.

——, CHEN, S. E., DAVIS, G. C., *et al* (1985) Borderline: an adjective in search of a noun. *Journal of Clinical Psychiatry*, **46**, 41–48.

—— & LEMMI, H. (1987) Sleep EEG findings bearing on the relationship of anxiety and depressive disorders. In *Anxious Depression: Assessment and Treatment* (eds G. Racagani & E. Smeraldi). New York: Raven Press.

—— & MALLYA, G. (1987) Criteria for the ''soft'' bipolar spectrum—treatment implications. *Psychopharmacology Bulletin*, **23**, 68–73.

—— & HAYKAL, R. F. (1988) Dysthymic and chronic depressive conditions. In *Depression and Mania: A Comprehensive Textbook* (eds A. Georgotas & R. Cancro), pp. 96–103. New York: Elsevier Publishing Co.

AMERICAN PSYCHIATRIC ASSOCIATION (1980) *Diagnostic and Statistical Manual of Mental Disorders* (3rd edn) (DSM–III). Washington, DC: APA.

—— (1987) *Diagnostic and Statistical Manual of Mental Disorders* (3rd edn, revised) (DSM–III–R). Washington, DC: APA.

ANGST, J. & DOBLER-MIKOLA, A. (1985) The Zurich Study. A prospective epidemiological study of depressive, neurotic and psychosomatic syndromes. IV. Recurrent and nonrecurrent brief depression. *European Archives of Psychiatry and Neurological Science*, **234**, 408–416.

AYD, F. J., JR (1984) Long-term treatment of chronic depression: 15-year experience with Doxepin HCl. *Journal of Clinical Psychiatry*, **45**, 39–46.

BERSANI, G., MARINI, S., GRISPINI, A., *et al* (1988) S_2-antagonism (ritanserin) in dysthymic disorder. *Psychopharmacology*, **96**, 244.

CASSANO, G. B., MAGGINI, C. & AKISKAL, H. (1983) Short-term, subchronic, and chronic sequelae of affective disorders. *Psychiatric Clinics of North America*, **6**, 55–67.

——, MUSETTI, L., PERUGI, G., *et al* (1988) A proposed new approach to the clinical subclassification of depressive illness. *Pharmacopsychiatria*, **21**, 19–23.

DELISIO, G., MAREMMANI, I., PERUGI, G., *et al* (1986) Impairment of work and leisure in depressed outpatients: a preliminary communication. *Journal of Affective Disorders*, **10**, 79–84.

HAURI, P. & SATEIA, M. J. (1984) REM sleep in dysthymic disorders. *Sleep Research*, **13**, 119.

HIRSCHFELD, R. M. A., KLERMAN, G. L., LAVORI, P., *et al* (1989) Premorbid personality assessments of first onset of major depression. *Archives of General Psychiatry*, **46**, 345–350.

KELLER, M. B., KLERMAN, G. L., LAVORI, P. W., *et al* (1982) Treatment received by depressed patients. *Journal of the American Medical Association*, **248**, 1848–1855.

——, LAVORI, P. W., ENDICOTT, J., *et al* (1983) "Double-depression": two-year follow-up. *American Journal of Psychiatry*, **140**, 689–694.

KLEIN, D. F., GITTELMAN, R., QUITKIN, F., *et al* (1980) *Diagnosis and Drug Treatment of Psychiatric Disorders: Adults and Children* (2nd edn). Baltimore: Williams & Wilkins.

——, TAYLOR, E. B., HARDING, K., *et al* (1988) Double depression and episodic major depression: demographic, clinical, familial, personality, and socioenvironmental characteristics and short-term outcome. *American Journal of Psychiatry*, **145**, 1226–1231.

KLERMAN, G. L., ENDICOTT, J., SPITZER, R., *et al* (1979) Neurotic depressions: a systematic analysis of multiple criteria and meanings. *American Journal of Psychiatry*, **136**, 57–70.

KOCSIS, J. H. & FRANCES, A. J. (1987) A critical discussion of DSM–III dysthymic disorder. *American Journal of Psychiatry*, **144**, 1534–1541.

——, ——, VOSS, C., *et al* (1988) Imipramine treatment for chronic depression. *Archives of General Psychiatry*, **45**, 253–257.

KOVACS, M. & GASTSONIS, C. (1989) Stability and change in childhood—Onset of depressive disorder: longitudinal course as a diagnostic validator. In *The Validity of Psychiatric Diagnosis* (eds L. N. Robins & J. E. Barrett), pp. 57–73. New York: Raven Press.

KRETSCHMER, E. (1936) *Physique and Character* (trans. E. Miller). London: Kegan Paul, Trench, Trubner and Co., Ltd.

LIEBOWITZ, M. R. & KLEIN, D. F. (1979) Hysteroid dysphoria. *Psychiatric Clinics of North America*, **2**, 555–575.

——, QUITKIN, F. M., STEWART, J. W., *et al* (1988) Antidepressant specificity in atypical depression. *Archives of General Psychiatry*, **45**, 129–137.

MCCULLOUGH, J. P. (1988) A longitudinal study of nonremitting and remitting subjects in an untreated sample of early-onset characterologic dysthymia. *Journal of Nervous and Mental Disease*, **176**, 658–667.

MECO, G., MARINI, S., MARIANI, L., *et al* (1988) Ritanserin in dysthymic disorders (DSM–III): a double-blind study versus amitriptyline. *Psychopharmacology*, **96**, 282.

MURPHY, D. & CHECKLEY, S. A. (1988) A prevalence study and treatment study of ritanserin in dysthymic disorder. *Psychopharmacology*, **96**, 109.

PRICE, J. S. (1978) Chronic depressive illness. *British Medical Journal*, *ii*, 1200–1201.

REYNTJENS, A. J. M., GELDERS, Y. G., HOPPENBROUWERS, M. L., *et al* (1986) Thymosthenic effects of ritanserin (R55667), a centrally acting serotonin-S, receptor blocker. *Drug Development Research*, **8**, 205–211.

ROSENTHAL, T. L., AKISKAL, H. S., SCOTT-STRAUSS, A., *et al* (1981) Familial and developmental factors in characterological depressions. *Journal of Affective Disorders*, **3**, 183–192.

SCHNEIDER, K. (1958) *Psychopathic Personalities* (trans. M. W. Hamilton). London: Cassell.

SCOTT, J., BARKER, W. A. & ECCLESTON, D. (1988) The Newcastle chronic depression study: patient characteristics and factors associated with chronicity. *British Journal of Psychiatry*, **152**, 28–33.

STEWART, J. W., QUITKIN, F. M., MCGRATH, P. J., *et al* (1988) Social functioning in chronic depression: effects of 6 weeks of antidepressant treatment. *Psychiatric Research*, **25**, 213–222.

VANVALKENBURG, C., LILIENFELD, B. A. & AKISKAL, H. S. (1987) The impact of familial personality disorder and alcoholism on the clinical features of depression. *Psychiatrie und Psychobiologie*, **11**, 195–201.

WARD, N. G., BLOOM, V. L. & FRIEDEL, R. O. (1979) The effectiveness of tricyclic antidepressants in chronic depression. *Journal of Clinical Psychiatry*, **40**, 49–52.

WEISSMAN, M. M. & KLERMAN, G. L. (1977) The chronic depressive in the community: unrecognized and poorly treated. *Comprehensive Psychiatry*, **18**, 523–532.

—— & AKISKAL, H. S. (1984) The role of psychotherapy in chronic depressions: a proposal. *Comprehensive Psychiatry*, **25**, 23–31.

WINOKUR, G. (1979) Unipolar depression—is it divisible into autonomous subtypes? *Archives of General Psychiatry*, **36**, 47–52.

WOOD, D. R., REIMHERR, F. W., WENDER, P. H., *et al* (1976) Diagnosis and treatment of minimal brain dysfunction in adults. *Archives of General Psychiatry*, **33**, 1453–1460.

2 Dysthymia: development and clinical course

M. B. KELLER and F. M. SESSA

The recognition of dysthymic disorder as a significant health problem is relatively new to psychiatry. Although there is a paucity of systematic studies of the nosology, clinical course of, and risk factors associated with dysthymia, epidemiological studies cite high prevalence rates of dysthymia in patient and non-patient samples. Data from the Epidemiologic Catchment Area (ECA) programme, which comprised an adult probability sample of five communities, showed a lifetime prevalence rate for dysthymia of 3.1% compared with a lifetime prevalence rate for major depression of 4.4% (Eaton & Kessler, 1985). The 1975 New Haven Survey found the lifetime rate of Research Diagnostic Criteria (RDC; Spitzer *et al*, 1978) chronic and intermittent depressive disorder (of at least two years' duration) was 4.5% (Weissman & Myers, 1978).

Defining dysthymia has been one problem contributing to the difficulty of studying the disorder. Although not synonymous, a variety of terms have been used to describe dysthymic disorder, including depressive temperament (Kraepelin, 1921; Kretschmer, 1936; Schneider, 1958), neurotic depression (DSM–II; American Psychiatric Association, 1968), depressive personality (Chodoff, 1972), hysteroid dysphoria (Liebowitz & Klein, 1979), characterological depression (Akiskal *et al*, 1980), and the RDC catcgories of chronic and intermittent depressive disorder and minor depressive disorder of at least two years' duration. As a result of studies showing the heterogeneous nature of neurotic depressions (Klein, 1974; Kendell, 1976; Akiskal *et al*, 1978; Klerman *et al*, 1979) and a decision to create a diagnostic category based only on phenomenology (Spitzer *et al*, 1980), DSM–III (American Psychiatric Association, 1980) introduced the term 'dysthymic disorder' to replace the DSM–II concept of neurotic depression in the American psychiatric nomenclature. An important aspect of this revision, which has been maintained with some modifications in DSM–III–R (American Psychiatric Association, 1987), is that dysthymia is included as an affective disorder rather than a personality disorder. (For further discussion of the 'definition' of dysthymia, the reader is referred to Chapter 1.)

Another factor related to the paucity of systematic research on dysthymia is the controversy over whether dysthymia and major depressive disorder represent distinct psychopathological disorders or are different phases of a single condition. The high comorbidity of dysthymia with major depression, as well as several other, non-affective disorders, has fueled this controversy. Based on data from the ECA programme, 70–75% of dysthymia cases coexist, over a lifetime, with other psychiatric disorders (Weissman *et al*, 1987).

With particular emphasis on the comorbidity of dysthymic disorder and major depressive disorder, this chapter addresses what is known about the development and clinical course of dysthymia. In attempting to answer the question of whether dysthymia and major depression are distinct entities or different phases of a single disorder, the relationship between dysthymia and major depression is explored, and data on the course of patients with dysthymia alone and those with major depression alone are compared with data on the course of patients with dysthymia and major depression.

Throughout this chapter, the term 'dysthymic disorder' (or 'dysthymia') is used as an inclusive label for chronic low-grade depression defined in DSM–III–R as dysthymia and in the RDC as chronic and intermittent depressive disorder and minor depressive disorder of at least two years' duration. The criteria for diagnosing chronic depression are similar in both systems of nomenclature.

The relationship between dysthymia and major depression

Diagnosis

The symptom criteria for dysthymia are similar to those for major depression. However, by definition, the presence of affective hallucinations and delusions and past or present episodes of mania or hypomania precludes the diagnosis of dysthymia. Although major depression can have an acute or chronic course, dysthymic disorder is characterised by chronicity: the persistent or intermittent depressive symptoms associated with dysthymia must have at least two years' duration. (In DSM–III–R the minimum duration of dysthymic disorder in children and adolescents is one year.) In addition, according to DSM–III–R, there should be no clear evidence of a major depressive episode during the first two years of the disturbance (one year for children and adolescents).

Dysthymia as prodromal to major depression

Suggesting that minor depressions form a foundation from which major affective episodes develop, Akiskal *et al* (1978) found that 36 out of 100 patients with neurotic depression developed melancholic episodes over three to four years. Akiskal *et al* (1981) reported that of 137 out-patients who were initially diagnosed as having DSM–III dysthymia approximately 90% had a course complicated by major affective episodes.

In a prospective study of 19 children with a diagnosis of dysthymia who were recruited from referrals to university-affiliated out-patient child psychiatric and paediatric clinics, Kovacs *et al* (1984*a*) found that more than 70% developed a major depressive episode during the first five years of follow-up.

Dysthymia as a residual syndrome

In a literature review by Klerman (1980) and in research by Keller *et al* (1984), Akiskal (1982), and Rounsaville *et al* (1980), at least 15–20% of patients with acute depressions do not completely recover, but instead show some intermittent, fluctuating chronic symptoms that frequently persist for years. Based on a retrospective study of 137 out-patients with dysthymia, Akiskal *et al* (1981) found that 28% of the sample developed chronic depression following an episode of major depression and 36% developed chronic depression as a complication of other psychiatric or medical disorders.

Based on the finding of an age difference in peak prevalence rates of dysthymia and major depression in subjects in the ECA study, Weissman *et al* (1988) hypothesise that dysthymia may be a residual syndrome of major depression. It appears, from their data, that the onset and highest risk periods for major depression are in young adulthood and for dysthymia in middle and older ages, suggesting "the dysthymia which remains in the older age groups may be the residuum of untreated major depression or partial recovery from a major depression". However, the authors temper this hypothesis by acknowledging that they cannot determine whether older subjects with dysthymia have had episodes of untreated major depression before their illness, since time of onset cannot be assessed with the ECA data.

Keller *et al* (1986) found a 15–20% rate of chronicity in successive cohorts with prospectively observed episodes of major depressive disorder following recovery from any episode of depression. This produces a 'silting' in the population which in all likelihood contributes to the proportion of patients who have been diagnosed as dysthymic.

Double depression

Although dysthymia does occur as a distinct disorder, it more frequently occurs simultaneously with other psychiatric disturbances, particularly major depressive disorder. Akiskal *et al* (1981) found that no more than 10% of out-patient probands in their study met DSM–III criteria for dysthymia in the absence of other psychiatric disorder. Further evidence of the clinical scarcity of subjects with 'pure' dysthymia comes from the National Institute of Mental Health (NIMH) Clinical Research Branch Program on the Psychobiology of Depression. After one and a half years, the investigators were able to recruit only nine such patients at five collaborating medical centres; further search for 'pure' dysthymic patients by these investigators at a variety of public and private out-patient facilities was as unsuccessful (Keller & Lavori, 1984).

Keller & Shapiro (1982) coined the term 'double depression' to describe the coexistence of acute episodes of major depression superimposed on dysthymia. In the NIMH Psychobiology of Depression Study, 25% of 316 patients with a major depressive disorder who were followed for between six months and two years had a pre-existing chronic minor depression of at least two years' duration (Keller *et al*, 1983). Rounsaville *et al* (1980) reported that 36% of 64 consecutively admitted patients who were diagnosed with RDC major depressive disorder also had an intermittent depressive disorder. In the ECA study (Weissman *et al*, 1988), nearly 39% of the subjects diagnosed with dysthymic disorder also met criteria for major depression.

In Kovacs *et al*'s (1984*a*) cohort of school-aged children, 93% of those with dysthymia had other concurrently diagnosed conditions, the most common being major depression (57%).

Natural course

Any discussion of the longitudinal course of dysthymia and major depression should be prefaced by stating that the majority of the published rates of recovery, recurrence, chronicity and predictors of outcome come from patients who sought treatment at medical and psychiatric treatment centres. It is therefore not clear how easy it is to generalise these data to the entire population of depressed patients, since a substantial proportion of people have depressive episodes which remit spontaneously, never seek treatment, or are treated in non-medical or non-psychiatric settings. Furthermore, most of the data on course are gleaned from naturalistic studies where the treatment received is not influenced by the research investigators; a high proportion of depressed patients seeking treatment at university medical centres received either minimal or no somatic treatment before entering these facilities despite being depressed for a median duration of six months (Keller *et al*, 1982). Surprisingly, even after patients were admitted to the treatment facilities, approximately 53% of out-patients received minimal or no antidepressant physical therapy during the first eight weeks, and 31% of the in-patients received minimal or no physical therapy during the two months (Keller *et al*, 1986).

Course of patients with dysthymia compared with that of patients with major depression

Recovery

Gonzales *et al* (1985) found significant differences in the recovery rates of patients with dysthymia and those with major depression after a one- to three-year interval following completion of a cognitive/behavioural intervention programme. The recovery rate for major depressives (75%) was significantly higher ($\chi^2 = 14.7$; $P<0.006$) than that of the intermittent depressives (43%). Based on self-report measures after a two-year interval, Barrett (1984) found a 37% rate of improvement among chronic depressives compared with a 72% rate for patients with major depression ($\chi^2 = 24.0$; $P<0.000$). Kovacs *et al* (1984*a*) found that the recovery rate for major depression was significantly better than for dysthymia in their school-age cohort (generalised Wilcoxon = 40.7; $P<0.0001$). They reported that it would take more than six years for the dysthymics to reach a maximal recovery rate of 89%, and for children in their study with major depression the maximal recovery rate of 92% was reached within one and a half years of the onset of the disorder.

Relapse

Gonzales *et al* (1985) found that the differences in the one-year relapse rates for chronic and intermittent depressed patients and for major depressives were not statistically significant. Within one year of recovery from entry into the study, the relapse rate for patients with chronic and intermittent depression was 33% compared with 31% for patients with major depression.

Chronicity

Rounsaville *et al* (1980) found an average duration of chronic and intermittent depression of 5.5 years (range 2–20 years) among chronically ill depressed out-patients. Keller *et al* (1982) reported similar findings: thcy found a median duration of five years for dysthymia before the first superimposition of an episode of major depression. Of the patients with an underlying depression, 96% had a chronic depression that lasted three years or more, 73% had a chronic depression that lasted five years or more, and 52% had a chronic depression that lasted ten years or more (Keller *et al*, 1982).

Pertaining to major depression, investigators have reported that between 10% and 20% of all patients diagnosed with major depression will have a chronic course (Robins & Guze, 1972; Murphy, 1974). Unpublished data from the NIMH Collaborative Depression Study indicate that 19% of unipolar depressed patients remained chronically ill after two years of a short-interval prospective follow-up, direct interview study, and 10% were still chronically ill after five years.

Kovacs *et al* (1984*a*) reported that the mean episode length of dysthymia and major depression was significantly different. Episodes of dysthymia were longer than episodes of major depression (3 years v. 32 weeks respectively).

Course of patients with double depression compared with that of patients with major depression alone

Recovery

When describing the recovery rates of patients with double depression, it is necessary to specify whether 'recovery' is defined as recovery from both the acute superimposed major depression and the underlying chronic depression or as recovery from only the major depression with a return to the patient's baseline chronic depressive state.

Keller & Shapiro (1982) report that the two-year recovery rates from major depression in patients with a double depression are significantly higher (97%) than the recovery rates from major depression alone in patients without an underlying chronic condition (79%). The authors stress that this finding does not imply that patients with a double depression become healthier than patients with a major depression alone, but rather that it is easier to return to a state of chronic, low-grade depression than to a state characterised by no depression.

According to patients' self-reports after two years of follow-up, Barrett (1984) found that patients with RDC major depressive disorder had a better outcome (100% improved) than patients with a superimposed major depression on an RDC chronic depressive disorder (100% no change or worse) ($\chi^2 = 48.3$; $P < 0.0000$). After one year of follow-up, Gonzales *et al* (1985) found a 27% recovery rate for patients with a double depression (when recovery was defined as a return to a usual self with no depressive symptoms at all) compared with a 75% recovery rate for patients with a major depression alone ($\chi^2 = 14.7$; $P < 0.006$). When the rate of recovery from double depression in Gonzales *et al*'s study was defined as recovery from the major depression alone, the one-year recovery rate was 65%.

In contrast to the differences in recovery rates between adult patients with double depression and those with major depression alone, Kovacs *et al* (1984*a*) found no significant differences between recovery from a major depression superimposed on dysthymia and recovery from a major depression without an underlying chronic depressive condition in their school-aged cohort.

Relapse

Keller *et al* (1983) found that patients with a double depression have a significantly higher rate of relapse by two years (58%) than patients with major depression alone (39%) ($P = 0.024$). Futhermore, patients with a double depression had a significantly faster cycle time for their major depression over two years of follow-up (Keller, 1985).

The longer a patient remains ill with an underlying dysthymia after recovering from the major depression, the greater is the likelihood that relapse into an episode of major depression will pre-empt recovery from the dysthymic disorder, based on life-table analyses (Keller *et al*, 1983). More specifically, after six months almost all patients with double depression in the NIMH Collaborative Depression Study relapsed into an episode of major affective disorder before they recovered from their chronic depression (Keller *et al*, 1983). Kovacs *et al* (1984*b*) found that the presence of an underlying dysthymia increased the risk of recurrent episodes of major depression.

Chronicity

Keller *et al* (1982) reported that of patients with an episode of RDC major depressive disorder who had a pre-existing low-grade depression of at least two years' duration, the duration of the underlying depression was three years or more in 96% of the patients, five years or more in 73%, and ten years or more in 42%.

Subtyping dysthymia

Because of the severity of course in patients with a double depression, investigators in the NIMH Psychobiology of Depression Study looked for clinical predictors of the speed of recovery from the major depression in patients with double depression. Looking at the sequential occurrence of dysthymia in patients with major depression, three groups of patients emerged: (a) patients whose dysthymia preceded their first major depression, and whose index episode of major depression was their first major depressive episode; (b) patients who had had more than one major depression, but whose dysthymia preceded the first episode of major depression; and (c) patients whose first episode of major depression came before their first dysthymia (Keller *et al*, unpublished data, 1984).

Unpublished data from Keller *et al* (data presented at the NIMH Workshop on Dysthmic Disorder in Washington, DC, 10–11 July 1986) indicate that patients whose dysthymia occurred first and who entered the study with their first episode of major depression had a significantly shorter time to recovery than patients in whom a major depression preceded their first dysthymia; and patients whose dysthymia occurred first and had at least two lifetime episodes of major depression had an outcome which was intermediate between these two groups. No association was found between outcome and the age of onset of the first dysthymia or the first major depression.

The retarded and psychotic subtypes of major depression were the only variables, characteristic of the index episode of major depression, with substantial predictive power: patients with retarded and psychotic major depression had longer times to recovery than patients with non-retarded and non-psychotic major depression. The primary and secondary subtypes of major depression were not significant predictors of outcome.

Speculating from these data, it can be hypothesised that patients whose major depression precedes their first dysthymia may represent a different type of double depression or chronic depression than patients whose dysthymia occurs first. This distinction may be a means of subtyping dysthymia, at least for the purpose of predicting future outcome.

Conclusion

During the past few years, there has been a growing interest in and the beginnings of a knowledge base about the development and course of dysthymia and its relationship to other disorders, especially major depression. Despite this attention, there have been few empirical studies of the course of dysthymia and most of these have had very small samples. Consequently, there is a paucity of knowledge on rates and predictors of recovery and relapse in dysthymia in adults and children.

To generate data describing the cross-sectional and long-term course of dysthymia and the multitude of pathways to chronicity in depressed patients, prospective longitudinal studies of dysthymia should be initiated. Non-clinically ascertained target populations might include individuals identified in epidemiological surveys as having dysthymia, children and young adults at risk for affective disorder based on having at least one parent with an affective illness, and individuals recruited because they are symptomatic 'volunteers' who are 'non-patients'. These long-term prospective follow-up studies will help to clarify the relationship between dysthymia and major depression, and provide information about factors unique to dysthymia in patients who do not go on to have episodes of major depression; this would give insight into the risk of developing major depression in dysthymic patients and help to describe homogeneous subtypes of dysthymia.

Moreover, while we await progress by researchers in psychopathology and nosology, there is an urgent need for treatment/intervention protocols which can modify this very pernicious disorder. We must begin to develop innovative treatment strategies to aid clinicians and patients. Such research must take into account the high rate of comorbidity found in patients with dysthymia and devise randomised clinical trials that recognise the 'real-life' heterogeneity of these conditions, rather than searching endlessly for rarefied homogeneous samples of pure dysthymic patients. Even if such subjects are collected, it will be difficult to generalise to people in the overall population who suffer from this illness contemporaneously with a multitude of other major psychiatric disorders and personality maladies.

Symposium discussion

PROFESSOR CASSANO: Do you have experience about generalised anxiety and depression as far as dysthymia is concerned and the relationship between those two disorders? We found a rather strong relationship between generalised anxiety and major depression which seemed to be like a double depression in some cases.

DR KELLER: I think there are two answers to this question. The short answer is no; the longer answer is that this relationship does exist, but, when we began our research in 1978, we used the RDC, in which anxiety states were essentially subsumed as being secondary or in some ways non-existent in the presence of a major depression. When we made a diagnosis, unless the anxiety state existed for six weeks before the onset of depression and persisted for six weeks afterwards, we did not diagnose anxiety.

A couple of years ago, when phobia and panic attracted much interest in the United States, people started coming back to us and asked whether we could reanalyse our data to look for anxiety symptoms. We are going back to looking at the symptoms which have been recorded in the structured clinical interview, the Schedule for Affective Disorder and Schizophrenia (SADS), and there is an extraordinary amount of anxiety present in the people with depression. Unfortunately, we are still trying to reconstruct a diagnosis of generalised anxiety.

However, we have moved on to do some other research specifically looking at the influence of depression on the comparative efficacy of treating various anxiety states, and I am finding that the percentage of comorbidity of anxiety in major depression and double depression is extraordinarily high. Probably 75% of people who have a major depressive disorder and almost everybody who also has a dysthymic disorder have a substantial number of anxiety symptoms. That is where we are at. Had you asked that question six or eight years ago, we would be a lot better off today.

References

AKISKAL, H. S. (1982) Factors associated with incomplete recovery in primary depressive illness. *Journal of Clinical Psychology*, **43**, 266–271.

——, BITAR, A. H., PUZANTIAN, M. D., *et al* (1978). The nosological status of neurotic depression: A prospective three-to-four year follow-up examination in light of the primary-secondary dichotomies. *Archives of General Psychiatry*, **35**, 756–766.

——, ROSENTHAL, T. L., HAYKAL, R. F., *et al* (1980) Characterological depressions: clinical and sleep EEG findings separating 'subaffective dysthymias' from 'character-spectrum disorders'. *Archives of General Psychiatry*, **37**, 777–783.

——, KING, D., ROSENTHAL, T. L., *et al* (1981) Chronic depression: Part I. Clinical and familial characteristics in 137 probands. *Journal of Affective Disorders*, **3**, 297–315.

AMERICAN PSYCHIATRIC ASSOCIATION (1968) *Diagnostic and Statistical Manual of Mental Disorders* (2nd edn) (DSM–II). Washington, DC: APA.

—— (1980) *Diagnostic and Statistical Manual of Mental Disorders* (3rd edn) (DSM–III). Washington, DC: APA.

—— (1987) *Diagnostic and Statistical Manual of Mental Disorders* (3rd edn, revised) (DSM–III–R). Washington, DC: APA.

BARRETT, J. E. (1984) Naturalistic change after 2 years in neurotic depressive disorders (RDC categories). *Comprehensive Psychiatry*, **25**, 404–418.

CHODOFF, K. (1972) The depressive personality. *Archives of General Psychiatry*, **27**, 666–673.

EATON, W. W. & KESSLER, L. G. (eds) (1985) *Epidemiological Field Methods in Psychiatry: The Epidemiological Catchment Area Program*. New York: Academic Press.

GONZALES, L. R., LEWINSOHN, P. M. & CLARKE, G. N. (1985) Longitudinal follow-up of unipolar depressives: an investigation of predictors of relapse. *Journal of Consulting and Clinical Psychology*, **53**, 461–469.

KELLER, M. B. (1985) Chronic and recurrent affective disorders: incidence, course and influencing factors. In *Chronic Treatments in Neuropsychiatry* (eds D. Kemali & G. Racagni). New York: Raven Press.

—— & SHAPIRO, R. W. (1982) "Double depression" superimposition of acute depressive episodes on chronic depressive disorders. *American Journal of Psychiatry*, **139**, 438–442.

——, KLERMAN, G. L., LAVORI, P. W., *et al* (1982) Treatment received by depressed patients. *Journal of the American Medical Association*, **248**, 1848–1855.

——, LAVORI, P. W., ENDICOTT, J., *et al* (1983) "Double depression": two-year follow-up. *American Journal of Psychiatry*, **140**, 689–694.

——, KLERMAN, G. L., LAVORI, P. W., *et al* (1984) Long-term outcome of episodes of major depression: clinical and public health significance. *Journal of the American Medical Association*, **252**, 788–792.

—— & LAVORI, P. W. (1984) Double depression, major depression, and dysthymia: distinct entities or different phases of a single disorder? *Psychopharmacology Bulletin*, **20**, 399–402.

——, ——, RICE, J., *et al* (1986) The persistent risk of chronicity in recurrent episodes of nonbipolar major depressive disorder. A prospective follow-up. *American Journal of Psychiatry*, **143**, 24–28.

KENDELL, R. E. (1976) The classification of depression: a review of contemporary confusion. *British Journal of Psychiatry*, **129**, 15–28.

KLEIN, D. F. (1974) Endogenomorphic depression: a conceptual and terminological revision. *Archives of General Psychiatry*, **31**, 447–454.

KLERMAN, G. L. (1980) Other specific affective disorders. In *Comprehensive Textbook of Psychiatry*, vol. 1 (3rd edn) (eds H. I. Kaplan & B. J. Sadock). Baltimore: Williams and Wilkins.

——, ENDICOTT, J., SPITZER, R., *et al* (1979) Neurotic depressions: a systematic analysis of multiple criteria and meanings. *American Journal of Psychiatry*, **136**, 57–61.

KOVACS, M., FEINBERG, T. L., CROUSE-NOVAK, M., *et al* (1984*a*) Depressive disorders in childhood: I. A longitudinal prospective study of characteristics and recovery. *Archives of General Psychiatry*, **41**, 229–237.

——, ——, ——, *et al* (1984*b*) Depressive disorders in childhood: II. A longitudinal study of risk for a subsequent major depression. *Archives of General Psychiatry*, **41**, 643–649.

KRAEPELIN, E. (1921) *Manic–Depressive Illness*. Edinburgh: E & S Livingstone, Ltd.

KRETSCHMER, E. (1936) *Physique and Character* (trans. E. Miller). London: Kegan Paul, Trench, Trubner and Co. Ltd.

LIEBOWITZ, M. R. & KLEIN, D. F. (1979) Hysteroid dysphoria. *Psychiatric Clinics of North America*, **2**, 555–575.

MURPHY, G. E. (1974) Variability of the clinical course of primary affective disorder. *Archives of General Psychiatry*, **30**, 757–761.

ROBINS, E. & GUZE, S. B. (1972) Classification of affective disorders: the primary–secondary, the endogenous and the neurotic–psychotic concepts. In *Recent Advances in the Psychobiology of Depressive Illness* (eds T. A. Williams, M. M. Katz & J. A Shield). Washington, DC: Department of Health, Education and Welfare.

ROUNSAVILLE, B. J., SHOLOMASKAS, D. & PRUSOFF, B. (1980) Chronic mood disorders in depressed outpatients: diagnosis and response to pharmacotherapy. *Journal of Affective Disorders*, **2**, 73–88.

SCHNEIDER, K. (1958) *Psychopathic Personalities* (trans. M. W. Hamilton). London: Cassell, Ltd.

SPITZER, R. L., ENDICOTT, J. & ROBINS, E. (1978) *Research Diagnostic Criteria (RDC) for a Selected Group of Functional Disorders*. New York: New York State Psychiatric Institute. (Updated in 1985.)

——, WILLIAMS, J. B. W. & SKODOL, A. E. (1980) DSM-III: The major achievements and an overview. *American Journal of Psychiatry*, **137**, 151–164.

WEISSMAN, M. M. & MYERS, J. K. (1978) Affective disorders in a US urban community: the use of research diagnostic criteria in an epidemiologic survey. *Archives of General Psychiatry*, **35**, 1304–1311.

——, LEAF, P. J., BRUCE, M. L., *et al* (1988) The epidemiology of dysthymia in the community: rates, risks, comorbidity and treatment. *American Journal of Psychiatry*, **145**, 815–819.

3 Relationship of dysthymia to anxiety and other neurotic disorders

N. SEIVEWRIGHT and P. TYRER

As outlined in Chapter 1, the specific diagnostic category of 'dysthymic disorder' is a creation of DSM–III (American Psychiatric Association, 1980), in which it was introduced instead of the DSM–II category of neurotic depression (American Psychiatric Association, 1968). As with the other diagnostic categories in this classification, the aim was to specify a group of particular clinical features, termed 'diagnostic criteria', which need to be present to apply the diagnostic label of dysthymic disorder. The DSM–III descriptions were introduced with the intention of improving consistency of diagnosis, with obvious advantages for communication and comparability of research work. Having specified the diagnostic criteria for each disorder, usually in the form of a range of symptoms, the classification also gives brief information on other clinical correlates such as age of onset, associated features, predisposing features and course, if such information is known.

The method of derivation of the categories in DSM–III and the need to keep apace with developing ideas and concepts inevitably mean that some diagnostic categories appear in the classification as a summary of a current consensus about a condition, with what amounts to working hypotheses about the various clinical aspects. A new category such as dysthymic disorder must be considered to be at this stage while research into clinical relationships, epidemiology, course and aetiological factors is undertaken.

Our interest in dysthymic disorder, as with other descriptions of the milder degrees of depression, is in the extent of overlap with anxiety disorders. A large body of evidence from studies of psychiatric patients, subjects from the general population and patients seen in general practice suggests that depressive and anxiety disorders are substantially or even inextricably linked, so that the validity of separating even the two broad types of disorder in psychiatric classification has been called into question (Tyrer, 1985). The study described here attempted to investigate the validity of the separate status of the diagnostic category of dysthymic disorder in two ways. Firstly, a group of patients with dysthymic disorder was compared with patients with two DSM–III-defined anxiety disorders on a number of clinical correlates which have been ascribed to dysthymic disorder in DSM–III and by previous research workers. Secondly, the longitudinal stability of the diagnosis of dysthymic disorder was investigated by repeating a diagnostic assessment on the former group at three regular intervals over 12 months.

Before describing the study, some of the evidence for a substantial overlap between depressive and anxiety disorders is briefly reviewed. Some of this evidence predates the introduction of the term 'dysthymic disorder' and relates to forms of the previous concept of 'neurotic depression'. The DSM–III definition of dysthymic disorder was intended to describe a narrower and less heterogeneous group of patients than was included in previous formalised or informal concepts of neurotic depression, and the features which are described as being characteristic of dysthymic disorder which this study investigates are also outlined.

Relationship between depressive and anxiety disorders

A popular view of this relationship, at least in the United Kingdom, is that the milder psychiatric disorders that are typically detected in health surveys or in general practice consultations frequently consist of a mixture of depressive and anxiety symptoms, but that disorders that come to the attention of psychiatrists appear to be more differentiated into one or other form, possibly meaning that illnesses that have become chronic or that are more severe are more easy to differentiate. However, there is evidence from across all the settings where psychiatric disorders are seen that the link between anxiety and depressive disorders is a strong one. Indeed in a study of psychiatric in-patients, Kendell (1974) found that of patients who had been admitted with a diagnosis of a neurotic disorder, less than 40% of patients who had another admission within the subsequent five years received the same diagnosis the next time around, compared with the equivalent figure of 75% for schizophrenia. Within the neurotic group, the proportion of people who were originally diagnosed as having 'reactive depression' who retained that diagnosis was only 34%, and the change of diagnosis from anxiety state to depression on readmission was one of the most frequently found relationships.

The studies of psychiatrically ill relatives of probands with depressive and anxiety disorders also shows the difficulty in separating these conditions as in general they cluster together in families. A particularly interesting study by Leckmann *et al* (1983) found that rates of DSM–III-defined major depressive disorders and anxiety disorders and rates of a combination of those disorders were all higher than expected in relatives of probands with combined depressive and anxiety disorders. A more straightforward approach by other researchers with psychiatric patients has been simply to monitor the coexistence of depressive and anxiety symptoms in patients with one or other 'main' diagnosis. In this way Bowen & Kohout (1979) found that 91% of a group of patients with a diagnosis of agoraphobia also met criteria for what he termed a primary affective disorder.

The coexistence of features of depression and anxiety in the disorders seen in general practice has been repeatedly demonstrated, notably in the studies of Goldberg and his colleagues (see Chapter 9). For instance in a study of 88 patients presenting with psychiatric illness in a general practice in Philadelphia (Goldberg & Huxley, 1980), the two commonest symptoms were anxiety or worry, present in 82 of the patients, and despondency or sadness, present in 71. These complaints had mostly occurred together and it was not possible to assign primacy to the anxiety or depressive component. Surveys have also provided evidence of similar overlap, such as that by Sashidharan *et al* (1985), who used the Research Diagnostic Criteria to diagnose women from a random sample who proved to have a psychiatric disorder. They found that it was commoner for the subjects' symptoms to qualify for both a depressive disorder and generalised anxiety disorder than to qualify for just one disorder, and also that a significant proportion of diagnoses changed during an 18-month prospective follow-up. The authors say that "we were impressed by the lack of specificity of the two most common diagnoses (depressive and anxiety disorder)".

Features of dysthymic disorder

As described in Chapter 1, the main symptoms required in DSM–III to make a diagnosis of dysthymic disorder are mildly depressed mood or substantial loss of interest, of long standing, specifically more than half of a two year period with no period free of those symptoms of more than three months. Any three of 13 other symptoms have also to be present, including insomnia, loss of energy, irritability, restlessness, pessimism about the future, tearfulness, and suicidal thoughts.

DSM–III is reasonably detailed about the characteristic associated clinical correlates of dysthymic disorder. Those that are the subject of comparisons made in this study are:

- mild depression of long standing (DSM–III)
- often young onset but may follow major depressive episode in older subjects (DSM–III; Akiskal, 1983)
- often associated personality disorder (DSM–III; Roy *et al*, 1985)
- often chronic psychological stressors (DSM–III)
- hospital admission rarely required unless there is associated major depressive episode or suicide attempt (DSM–III)
- chronic course (DSM–III; Akiskal, 1983; Keller, see Chapter 2).

The age at onset is said in DSM–III to be "usually early in adult life [but] it may begin at a period later in adulthood, in some instances following a Major Depression''. Akiskal (1983), in an article proposing four subtypes of dysthymic disorder, also suggests that onset is usually early but that if the condition constitutes the residual effects of a major depression or if it is secondary to other psychiatric or physical disorder then onset may be later.

The account in DSM–III states that ''often an associated personality disturbance warrants an additional diagnosis of a personality disorder on Axis II''. In a study of 11 dysthymic disorder patients Roy *et al* (1985) considered on clinical assessment that nine had an associated personality disorder that met DSM–III criteria as opposed to none of a group of 11 age- and sex-matched control subjects. The nine personality disorder diagnoses consisted of four borderline, two schizoid, one histrionic, one compulsive and one dependent.

Another predisposing factor according to DSM–III is the presence of ''chronic psychosocial stressors''. As far as we are aware no study of life events has been undertaken in dysthymic disorder, although there is much evidence relating life events and ongoing psychosocial 'difficulties' to other definitions of depression (Paykel *et al*, 1969; Brown & Harris, 1978; Surtees *et al*, 1986), and indeed to anxiety disorders (Finlay-Jones & Brown, 1981).

Since dysthymic disorder is basically a mild condition it is stated in the DSM–III account that ''hospitalization is rarely required unless there is a suicide attempt or a superimposed major affective disorder''.

Finally, of the features considered in our prospective study, the course of dysthymic disorder is described in DSM–III simply as ''chronic''. The account by Akiskal (1983) considers that chronicity is by definition a feature of the proposed subgroup who remain mildly depressed after a major depressive episode, and he describes controlled comparisons with episodically depressed patients which found that chronicity was related to ''heredofamilial affective loading, multiple losses through death of family members, disabled spouses or other family members, the use of depressant anti-hypertensive agents, and secondary drug dependence''. He considers that dysthymic conditions that are secondary to other psychiatric or physical disorders vary with the underlying condition, and that the remainder, consisting of early-onset dysthymic disorders, may be intermittent or continuous. The studies by Keller of the course of dysthymic disorder are detailed in Chapter 2. Two striking findings from that work were that dysthymic disorder has a substantially lower recovery rate than major depression and that dysthymic disorder is invariably complicated by the development of episodes of major depression. Whether the development of other psychiatric syndromes complicates the course of dysthymic disorder has not been studied in the same way and such an investigation forms the second part of this study.

A comparison of patient characteristics in dysthymic disorder, generalised anxiety disorder and panic disorder

Subjects

The group of subjects consisted of all patients presenting at one consultant's (PT's) out-patient clinics in a four-year period who met DSM–III criteria for dysthymic disorder, generalised anxiety disorder or panic disorder and at the time of assessment were having no treatment. Patients with a past history of melancholia, mania or schizophrenia were excluded. All patients were entered into a study in which they were randomly allocated irrespective of diagnosis to a short course of drug treatment, in the form of dothiepin, diazepam, or placebo (again randomly allocated and using a double-blind procedure), cognitive and behaviour therapy, or a self-help package. The early results of the treatment study have been reported (Tyrer *et al*, 1988), while the longer-term results will be reported in due course.

Study interviews

The DSM–III diagnosis of the patients' condition was made by administration by one author (PT) of the Structured Clinical Interview for DSM–III (SCID; Spitzer & Williams, 1983). This schedule is in two parts. The first part collects the following information: demographic data; duration of illness; details of any events occurring at the time of the onset of illness; and previous psychiatric treatment. The second part incorporates the diagnostic criteria of DSM–III into the form of a clinical interview so that a diagnosis can be made that exactly corresponds to the criteria.

Two other interviews were undertaken at the start of the study. In order to take account of more recent life events which might be more relevant to the degree of ongoing stress than the initial precipitating events, a 61-item life events questionnaire (Paykel *et al*, 1971), widely used in previous studies, was administered, covering the previous six months. In addition, pre-morbid personality was assessed using the Personality Assessment Schedule (Tyrer & Alexander, 1979), a recently devised structured interview which has been demonstrated to give a reliable and valid measure of pre-morbid personality even in the presence of additional psychiatric disorder (Tyrer *et al*, 1983). This schedule establishes a diagnosis of either normal personality or one of the four personality disorders that have proved to be clinically distinct in cluster analyses of the results from use of the schedule: sociopathic, passive-dependent, anankastic and schizoid personality disorders. These two additional interviews were undertaken in each case by one of a team of five raters, all psychiatrists trained in the use of both schedules. None of the raters was aware of the nature of this study.

Results

Results are presented here of the patients seen in the first three years of the study. Over this period 159 patients presented with one of the three diagnoses required for the study and were receiving no treatment: 48 with dysthymic disorder, 50 with generalised anxiety disorder and 61 with panic disorder.

TABLE 3.1
Demographic characteristics of patients with dysthymia, generalised anxiety disorder (GAD) and panic disorder

	Dysthymia (n = *48*)	*GAD* (n = *50*)	*Panic disorder* (n = *61*)
Mean age at onset: years	34.1 (s.d. 12.3)	33.9 (s.d. 12.8)	33.1 (s.d. 12.3)
Sex			
male	13	14	23
female	35	36	38
Marital status			
single	12	21	17
married	21	18	23
separated/divorced/widowed	15	11	21
Social class			
I–III	15	15	25
IV, V	33	35	36

Differences are not significant using (except for age) χ^2 test.

TABLE 3.2
Precipitating life events in patients with dysthymia, generalised anxiety disorder (GAD) and panic disorder

	Dysthymia (n = *48*)	*GAD* (n = *50*)	*Panic disorder* (n = *61*)
None	6	7	19
Illness/death events	17	14	14
Marital/children/opposite sex events	16	14	15
Work/education events	4	7	5
Other events	5	8	8

$\chi^2 = 9.91$, NS.
A comparison of patients who had no precipitating events with patients who had any kind of event shows that more patients with panic disorder had no precipitants, $\chi^2 = 7.51$, d.f. = 2, $P<0.025$.

Demographic characteristics

These are presented in Table 3.1. The age at onset of psychiatric disorder was calculated from age at study entry and duration of illness and the means and standard deviations were remarkably similar for all three diagnoses. All three diagnoses were commoner in women and there was no significant difference between the three groups in sex ratios. Neither were there significant differences between the groups in terms of marital status or distribution of social class.

Precipitating life events

These data are presented in Table 3.2. Numbers of patients who said that there had been no precipitating life events and of patients who had had life events at the time of onset of their illness are shown. The events have been grouped into combinations of the categories devised by Paykel and colleagues

TABLE 3.3
Life events in the six months before study entry in patients with dysthymia, generalised anxiety disorder (GAD) and panic disorder

	Dysthymia (n = *48*)	*GAD* (n = *50*)	*Panic disorder* (n = *61*)
Mean number of life events	2.88	2.66	2.75
Mean score of life events	30.99	27.93	30.62

Differences are not significant.

TABLE 3.4
Previous psychiatric treatment status of patients presenting with dysthymia, generalised anxiety disorder (GAD) and panic disorder

	Dysthymia (n = *48*)	*GAD* (n = *50*)	*Panic disorder* (n = *61*)
None	20	23	30
Out-patient/day-patient treatment	18	18	22
In-patient treatment	10	9	9

$\chi^2 = 9.20$, NS.

(Paykel *et al*, 1969; Jacobs *et al*, 1974), combinations rather than single categories being used because of the relatively small numbers of events involved. There were no significant differences between the three diagnostic groups in the patterns of precipitating life events. When a simpler comparison was made between those who had no precipitating events and those who had had any kind of precipitating events, significantly more patients with panic disorder had had no events ($\chi^2 = 7.51$, d.f. = 2, $P < 0.025$).

Recent life events

These data are presented in Table 3.3. In the six months before study entry the mean number of life events contained in the questionnaire that had been experienced by patients in each of the diagnostic groups was a little under three. The rates did not differ significantly. Because the process of simply counting the numbers of events experienced means that the most severe and stressful events count the same as the most minor events and differences between the groups in the degree of stress involved might be obscured, the consensus-derived scores contained in the schedule attached to each event indicating its degree of stressful intensity were also analysed. However, the mean scores for the three diagnostic groups also did not differ significantly.

Previous psychiatric treatment status

The hypothesis regarding hospitalisation was tested using information obtained in the SCID interview. Table 3.4 shows the numbers of those

TABLE 3.5

Personality diagnoses in patients with dysthymia, generalised anxiety disorder (GAD) and panic disorder

	Dysthymia (n = *48)*	*GAD* (n = *50)*	*Panic disorder* (n = *61)*
Non-disordered personality	26	31	44
Sociopathic personality	10	9	9
Passive-dependent personality disorder	6	4	4
Anankastic personality disorder	4	6	3
Schizoid personality disorder	2	0	1

$\chi^2 = 7.07$, NS whole table.
$\chi^2 = 3.81$, NS for comparison using non-disordered personality/personality disorder only.

TABLE 3.6

Duration of illness in patients presenting with dysthymia, generalised anxiety disorder (GAD) and panic disorder

	Dysthymia (n = *48)*	*GAD* (n = *50)*	*Panic disorder* (n = *61)*
0–6 months	2[1]	11	23
6–12 months	5[1]	14	10
12–24 months	10	9	7
>24 months	31	16	21

Dysthymia v. GAD, $z = -4.09$, $P<0.00001$.
Dysthymia v. panic disorder, $z = -3.96$, $P<0.0001$.
(Mann–Whitney *U* tests.)
1. Duration is for present episode only: previous episodes allow these patients to qualify for the diagnosis.

patients in the three diagnostic groups who had previously had no psychiatric treatment as an out-patient or day patient and no hospital admissions. No significant differences between the groups in the status of previous treatment were found.

Personality assessments

The personality diagnoses established by administration of the Personality Assessment Schedule to all patients are shown in Table 3.5. Between one-half and three-quarters of patients in each of the three diagnostic groups were diagnosed as having a normal, non-disordered personality. In the patients diagnosed as having a personality disorder, sociopathic personality was the most frequent type in all three groups, schizoid personality the least frequent in all three groups, with passive-dependent and anankastic personality disorders in between. Statistical comparisons of the range of personality diagnoses between the three groups showed no significant differences. A simpler comparison between those who had a normal personality and those who had a personality disorder of any type also failed to show significant differences between the three groups.

Duration of illness

These data are presented in Table 3.6. This is the only comparison which showed a clear-cut distinction between the three diagnostic groups. Patients with dysthymic disorder were significantly more likely to have had long-standing illness than patients with generalised anxiety disorder or panic disorder. This is clearly a reflection of the DSM–III diagnostic criteria for the three conditions: the diagnosis of dysthymic disorder requires a duration of symptoms of most of the previous two years, whereas the equivalent criteria for generalised anxiety disorder is most of the previous six months, and that for panic disorder just three weeks. It may be noted from Table 3.6 that seven patients in the dysthymic group had an illness duration of less than 12 months, which apparently does not reach the threshold for making that diagnosis. This however is because the initial SCID question on duration of illness refers to the current episode of illness only, which was short in these patients, but a subsequent question established that they had had previous similar symptoms which when taken together added up to most of the past two years without more than a three-month gap, hence qualifying for the diagnosis.

The course of dysthymic disorder

The course of dysthymic disorder was investigated in a prospective study by a straightforward method. Four, eight and twelve months after study entry the group of patients initially diagnosed as having dysthymic disorder were seen again by one of the rating team and the SCID diagnostic interview was repeated. As with the other interviews, all raters had been fully trained in the use of this schedule and were unaware of the nature of this study. The results of the diagnostic assessments at four, eight and twelve months after the initial diagnosis of dysthymic disorder are shown in Table 3.7. Some patients were lost to follow-up (6 at 4 months, 11 in total at 8 months and 12 in total at 12 months). Of the remainder a diagnosis of dysthymic disorder was retained in a relatively small number of patients. At four months, 11 out of 42 patients (26%) were diagnosed as still having dysthymic disorder, 9 (21%) had improved to the extent that they had no psychiatric disorder, but over half had developed a different DSM–III disorder. Major depressive episode was the commonest of these, more subjects having developed this condition than retained the diagnosis of dysthymia. The other diagnoses at four months were all anxiety disorders: in order of frequency panic disorder, generalised anxiety disorder, agoraphobia and social phobia.

At eight months a rather similar situation applied. By then a third of patients had improved enough to warrant no psychiatric diagnosis. Eight subjects (22%) had retained the diagnosis of dysthymia, and the same number had developed a major depressive episode. The diagnoses of generalised anxiety disorder, agoraphobia and panic disorder accounted for

TABLE 3.7
DSM–III diagnoses made by SCID interviews at 4, 8 and 12 months in patients initially diagnosed as having dysthymic disorder

SCID diagnosis	*No. with diagnosis*		
	4 months (n = *42*)	*8 months* (n = *37*)	*12 months* (n = *36*)
Major depressive episode	12	8	9
Dysthymia	11 (26%)	8 (22%)	4 (11%)
Generalised anxiety disorder	2	3	3
Melancholia	—	—	2
Panic disorder	5	2	1
Agoraphobia	2	3	—
Obsessive–compulsive disorder	—	—	1
Social phobia	1	—	1
Simple phobia	—	—	1
Schizophreniform disorder	—	1	—
No psychiatric disorder	9 (21%)	12 (32%)	14 (39%)

another eight subjects, and one subject's symptoms had gone out of the neurotic field and constituted a schizophreniform disorder.

At 12 months a higher proportion still had improved, 14 out of 36 (39%). By this stage only four subjects still retained a diagnosis of dysthymic disorder, which once again meant that half the subjects had developed a different disorder. Major depressive episode was again the commonest diagnosis, in nine subjects, and another two subjects had developed melancholia. The remaining diagnoses at 12 months were generalised anxiety disorder in three subjects and panic disorder, obsessive–compulsive disorder, social phobia and simple phobia, all in one subject each.

Implications of the study findings

The main objective of the study was to investigate the validity of the separate status of dysthymic disorder from anxiety disorders, tested in both parts of the study, and from other neurotic and depressive disorders, tested in the second prospective part of the study. In undertaking the comparisons made in the first part of the study it was also possible to test some of the statements made about dysthymic disorder in DSM–III and by previous researchers. The comparisons were chosen for that reason: because they investigated features said to be characteristic of dysthymia. Also the data presented here represent all the data we had on these dysthymic patients and anxious patients. Therefore it might have been expected that some differences between the three groups in terms of these clinical correlates were to emerge. On the whole however the uniformity between the groups was striking: of all the comparisons made, the only significant difference between dysthymia and the other groups was in duration of illness, and as explained above that is clearly a consequence of the diagnostic 'rules' which require more than 12 months of symptoms (over two years) before the diagnosis can be used.

Turning to the findings in the dysthymic group which can be compared with previous statements made about dysthymic disorder, two might be considered surprising. One was that 10 out of 48 dysthymic patients had required admission to hospital. This is in the context of a psychiatric service in which community-care facilities are well developed and admission reserved for serious conditions, and could mean that the complications requiring admission mentioned in DSM–III may be frequent in this group. The other was that when reliable formal assessments of personality were undertaken under blind conditions the coexistence of an Axis II diagnosis of personality disorder was present in under half the patients, which contrasts with the higher rate found by Roy *et al* (1985) in a small study under different conditions. Our dysthymic patients tended to be young at onset, female, from lower socio-economic groups, and to have had life events both at the onset of disorder and more recently before an interview. However, they did not differ from anxious patients in these or the above respects, and the overwhelming finding from the comparative analyses is that our results do not support the separation of dysthymic disorder from anxiety disorders on these clinical correlates.

The findings of the follow-up part of the study also point to substantial overlap of dysthymia with other conditions. The proportion of subjects whose symptoms still constituted the criteria for dysthymia four months after initial diagnosis was only just over a quarter, falling to just four out of 36 one year on. A significant number of patients were lost to research follow-up in the later stages but there is no compelling reason to think that the proportions of those who had retained the diagnosis, improved, or developed a different diagnosis would be greatly different from those who were followed up, and anyway the four-month follow-up was on all but six.

The patients did of course take part in a treatment study, but the main treatment course lasted just six weeks, with additional treatment if necessary in some patients, and it is our view that treatment cannot be considered a major factor. An extreme interpretation of the findings could be that all the improvements were due to treatment and all the changes of diagnosis from dysthymia to a diagnosis lower down the DSM–III diagnostic 'hierarchy', such as generalised anxiety disorder, could be because the subject initially had both types of symptoms and so the diagnosis of dysthymia took precedence, and that at follow-up treatment had removed the dysthymic symptoms and 'left' a diagnosis of generalised anxiety disorder. In reality this is extremely unlikely, and at any rate most changes of diagnosis were to diagnoses higher up the diagnostic hierarchy. The inescapable conclusion seems to be that other major depressive and neurotic symptoms are so closely linked with dysthymic symptoms that the diagnosis of dysthymic disorder is not one which has a high degree of longitudinal stability.

The results of the whole study combining clinical correlates with symptoms measured prospectively do not support the separate diagnostic status of dysthymic disorder and at this stage the boundaries of this new diagnostic category must be considered unclear.

Symposium discussion

DR BERGMAN: May I ask if the 11% at the 12-month survey who were dysthymic were dysthymic all the time or were there some people who had become dysthymic who were previously non-dysthymic and had other diagnoses?

DR SEIVEWRIGHT: We do not actually know that from these figures—the figures just give the breakdown of diagnosis over these periods. This is part of ongoing work and since I am really presenting preliminary findings, we do not know if they are the same patients.

DR BERGMAN: So you do not know if they are core dysthymics or not.

DR SEIVEWRIGHT: Unfortunately not from these data.

DR HALE: What was the stability of generalised anxiety disorders and the panic disorders on your one-year follow-up? Was that similarly unstable?

DR SEIVEWRIGHT: We have not analysed the data on anxiety and panic disorders yet.

References

AKISKAL, H. S. (1983) Dysthymic disorder: psychopathology of proposed chronic depressive subtypes. *American Journal of Psychiatry*, **140**, 11–22.

AMERICAN PSYCHIATRIC ASSOCIATION (1968) *Diagnostic and Statistical Manual of Mental Disorders* (2nd edn) (DSM–II). Washington, DC: APA.

—— (1980) *Diagnostic and Statistical Manual of Mental Disorders* (3rd edn) (DSM–III). Washington, DC: APA.

BOWEN, R. C. & KOHOUT, J. (1979) The relationship between agoraphobia and primary affective disorders. *Canadian Journal of Psychiatry*, **24**, 317–322.

BROWN, G. W. & HARRIS, T. (1978) *Social Origins of Depression*. London: Tavistock.

FINLAY-JONES, R. & BROWN, G. W. (1981) Types of stressful life event and the onset of anxiety and depressive disorders. *Psychological Medicine*, **11**, 803–815.

GOLDBERG, D. & HUXLEY, P. (1980) *Mental Illness in the Community: the Pathway to Psychiatric Care* (ch. 4). London: Tavistock.

JACOBS, S. C., PRUSOFF, B. A. & PAYKEL, E. S. (1974) Recent life events in schizophrenia and depression. *Psychological Medicine*, **4**, 444–453.

KENDELL, R. E. (1974) The stability of psychiatric diagnoses. *British Journal of Psychiatry*, **124**, 352–356.

LECKMAN, J. F., MERIKANGAS, K. R., PAULS, D. L., *et al* (1983) Anxiety disorders and depression: contradictions between family study data and DSM–III conventions. *American Journal of Psychiatry*, **140**, 880–882.

PAYKEL, E. S., MYERS, J. K., DIENELT, M. N., *et al* (1969) Life events and depression: a controlled study. *Archives of General Psychiatry*, **21**, 753–760.

——, PRUSOFF, B. A. & UHLENHUTH, E. H. (1971) Scaling of life events. *Archives of General Psychiatry*, **25**, 340–347.

ROY, A., SUTTON, M. & PICKAR, D. (1985) Neuroendocrine and personality variables in dysthymic disorder. *American Journal of Psychiatry*, **142**, 94–97.

SASHIDHARAN, S. P., SURTEES, P. G., INGHAM, J. G., *et al* (1985) Neurosis divisible? *Lancet*, *i*, 1210.

SPITZER, R. L. & WILLIAMS, J. B. W. (1983) *Structured Clinical Interview for DSM-III*. New York: New York State Institute.

SURTEES, P. G., MILLER, P. McC., INGHAM, J. G., *et al* (1986) Life events and the onset of affective disorder, a longitudinal general population study. *Journal of Affective Disorders*, **10**, 37–50.

TYRER, P. (1985) Neurosis divisible? *Lancet*, *i*, 685–688.

—— & ALEXANDER, J. (1979) Classification of personality disorder. *British Journal of Psychiatry*, **135**, 163–167.

——, STRAUSS, J. & CICCHETTI, D. (1983) Temporal reliability of personality in psychiatric patients. *Psychological Medicine*, **13**, 393–398.

——, SEIVEWRIGHT, N., MURPHY, S., *et al* (1988) The Nottingham Study of neurotic disorder: comparison of drug and psychological treatments. *Lancet*, *ii*, 235.

4 Dysthymia presenting to the Emergency Clinic at the Maudsley Hospital

D. MURPHY and S. A. CHECKLEY

The concept of dysthymia arose from an attempt to identify a relatively homogeneous group of patients from within the heterogeneous group covered by the term 'depressive neurosis'. The heterogeneity of such patients is particularly evident in follow-up studies (Akiskal *et al*, 1978). However, within the heterogeneous group a small subgroup can be identified who, over time, retain the characteristic features of depressive neurosis.

Akiskal *et al* (1978) proposed that the distinction between dysthymia (chronic depressive neurosis) and major depression is validated by clinical characteristics that are independent of clinical outcome. Akiskal (1983) then further subdivided dysthymia in a two-stage manner. In the first stage he divided it into three major types: (a) late onset, primary depression with residual chronicity, (b) variable-onset chronic secondary dysphorias, and (c) early-onset characterological depression. In the second stage he further divided the early-onset characterological group into subaffective dysthymic disorder (SDD) and character spectrum disorder (CSD). A case-note study suggested that one subgroup (SDD) had responded to antidepressant drug treatment whereas the other (CSD) had not. Akiskal argued that SDD represented a minor form of affective disorders whereas CSD represented a form of personality disorder. In support of such a distinction, Akiskal *et al* (1980) reported that patients with SDD have a short rapid eye movement (REM) latency, more continuous dysphoria, a positive family history for unipolar or bipolar depression and depressive personality characteristics as described by Schneider (1958). (See also Chapter 1.)

In contrast, patients with CSD were reported to be more commonly women, to have normal REM latencies, more intermittent dysphoria, positive family histories for alcoholism, a developmental history characterised by parental separation and a dependent histrionic or sociopathic personality (Akiskal *et al*, 1980, 1981; Rosenthal *et al*, 1981; Akiskal, 1983). Furthermore, whereas SDD was thought to begin in adult life before the age of 25, CSD was thought to begin in childhood or adolescence.

The aim of the present study was to test the validity of the distinctions both between dysthymia and major depression and also between SDD and CSD. Depressed patients were classified using Akiskal's operational criteria. The groups were then compared in terms of the clinical characteristics that have been reported to differentiate between the groups. It will be seen that the distinction between dysthymia and major depression is confirmed but that the distinction between SDD and CSD is not.

Method

All consecutive self, general practitioner, hospital, or other referrals to the Maudsley Hospital Emergency Clinic over three months were screened clinically for depression. If dysphoria or depression was suspected, a semistructured interview was carried out, and diagnosis assigned using the DSM–III criteria (American Psychiatric Association, 1980) for major depressive episode, melancholia, cyclothymia, generalised anxiety disorder, phobias and dysthymia. Personality disorder was assessed using both Schneider's depressive typology (Schneider, 1958) and DSM–III. Feighner *et al*'s (1972) criteria were used to exclude non-affective disorder. However, patients were included with diagnoses of drug and alcohol abuse and generalised anxiety disorder if two informants confirmed that these states had developed after five years of dysthymia. Severity of symptoms was measured using the Hamilton Rating Scales for Depression (HRSD; Hamilton, 1960) and Anxiety (HRSA; Hamilton, 1959).

In all cases information was gathered from at least one other informant to substantiate the patient's historical recall. In addition to this, and to ensure that self-report for dysthymic criteria was not affected by a depressive cognitive set, all patients diagnosed as having a 'double depression' (i.e. dysthymia and depression) were followed up for at least one month after the cessation of the major depressive episode. If at follow-up criteria for dysthymia were no longer fulfilled, the subject was reallocated to the appropriate diagnostic category.

Dysthymics were subdivided into those with late onset (primary depression with residual chronicity), variable onset (chronic secondary dysphorias) and early onset (characterological dysthymics and subaffective dysthymics) using Akiskal's (1983) operational criteria.

In order to investigate the characteristics that distinguished dysthymic patients from the major affectives, multivariate analyses of variance were performed. The first aim was to find the relevant variables in classifying depressed patients as major affective, dysthymic or 'other'. Further aims were to select the relevant variables in classifying dysthymic patients as having either character spectrum disorders or subaffective disorders, and as having pure dysthymia or double depression. By using the techniques of discriminant analysis and canonical variate analysis, some idea of the separation or overlap between the groups of patients can be gained. New patients could be classified using only the variables selected by discriminant analysis: an estimate of the proportion of correct classifications was found.

Discriminant analysis

Program P7M of the statistical package BMDP was used. The analysis seeks the subset of variables that discriminates best between the groups. This is done in steps, selecting one variable at a time. At each step, every variable is tested for inclusion in a function which expresses the difference between the groups. An F-statistic is calculated for each variable, and the variable with the largest F-statistic is selected. The program then proceeds to the next step. When none of the variables not yet selected has a large enough F-statistic ($F = 4.00$) to be included, the analysis is complete.

Discriminant analysis not only selects the variables that discriminate between the groups, it can also be used to estimate the proportion of new patients who would be correctly classified if the selected variables *only* were used in the classification procedure.

Canonical variate analysis

A measure of the separation of the groups of patients is given using canonical variate analysis. The selected variables (as identified by discriminant analysis) are transformed linearly and projected onto a subspace in such a way as to emphasise the differences between the groups as much as possible. This can be done in the form of a scatter plot if there are three groups or a histogram if there are two groups. Each patient is represented individually in these diagrams and any overlap between groups can be seen clearly.

Variables

From all the information collected on each patient, a list of variables was drawn up, which according to the literature might distinguish between the diagnostic entities under study. The list of variables is given below.

Age (years)
Sex
Disorder (major affective, dysthymic or other)
  for dysthymics only: CHD/SUB group or PD/DD group
Age of onset (years)
Hamilton depression score
Dysthymic criteria (yes/no to each of 13 questions)
Schneiderian depressive typology
Generalised anxiety disorder (yes/no)
Hamilton anxiety score

Number of past affective episodes
Number of hospital admissions
Number of overdoses
Number of hypomanic episodes
Alcohol abuse (yes/no)
Regular tranquilliser (yes/no)
Family history of DSM–III categories in first-degree relatives:
  affective parent only
  alcoholic parent only
  alcohol (1 parent) + affective (other parent)
  alcohol + affective (other relatives)
  affective + other (not alcohol) e.g. drug abuse/schizophrenia
Medication/drug abuse
Phobias (yes/no)
Personality disorder (yes/no, type)
Marital status (single, married or living with someone, widowed)
Marital stability (no. of separations or divorces)
Number of legitimate children
Number of illegitimate children
Number of terminations
Present employment (yes/no/housewife)
Past employment (yes/no/housewife)
Longest period unemployed (years)
Longest period employed (years)
School truant (yes/no)
Passed any official examinations (yes/no)
Age left school/full-time education
Number of close friends currently
Number of past convictions for 'violent' crimes
Number of past convictions for 'non-violent' crimes
Experiences before age 15:
  loss of parent by death (yes/no)
  parents separated or divorced (yes/no)
  adopted (yes/no)
  illegitimate (yes/no)
  illegitimate and separated from parents (yes/no)
Constancy of mood: intervals of normal mood for 1 week 'sometimes', 'often' or 'never'

In addition to Akiskal's (1983) criteria, a further refinement of the dysthymic group was attempted by comparing those who presented in a 'double depression' to those who complained of 'pure' dysthymic symptoms ('double depression' refers to the coincidence of major depression and dysthymia).

TABLE 4.1
Comparison of patients with dysthymia with those with major affective episode

	Dysthymia (n = *24*)	*Major affective episode* (n = *20*)	*Statistical significance*
Mean age at interview: years ± s.d.	31.4 (± 10.3)	39.9 (± 13.1)	*t*-test $P<0.02$
Mean age at onset: years ± s.d.	17.4 (± 7.2)	36.4 (± 12.9)	*t*-test $P<0.001$
% female	25%	50%	$P=0.12$
Mean Hamilton depression score (± s.d.)	15.2 (± 4.8)	17.3 (± 4.3)	
Mean Hamilton anxiety score (± s.d.)	14.1 (± 7.0)	8.8 (± 4.8)	*t*-test $P=0.006$
Past affective illness[1]	85%	45%	Fisher's $P=0.004$
Past overdoses	37%	5%	Fisher's $P=0.01$
Past admissions to psychiatric hospital	24%	10%	NS
DSM-III criteria for personality disorder	33%	25%	NS
Mean no. of legitimate children	0.39 (± 0.78)	1.15 (± 1.57)	NS
Parents separated by divorce	54%	5%	$P<0.001$
No. of experiences of separation before age 15:			
0	33%	85%	$\chi^2 = 12.6$
1	46%	15%	d.f. = 2
3	21%	0%	$P=0.002$
Family history of:			
alcoholism only	20%	5%	NS
affective disorder only	12%	50%	Fisher's $P=0.009$
affective disorder and alcoholism*	24%	15%	NS
affective disorder and other	12%	0%	NS

*Fisher's exact test (2-tail) for presence alcoholism alone or in combination with other psychiatric disorder, $P=0.11$.

1. DSM-III criteria.

Results

Dysthymia compared with major affective episode

The following statistically significant differences were found between patients categorised as major affective episode and dysthymia (see also Table 4.1).

(a) Patients with dysthymia had higher scores in the HRSA ($P=0.006$, paired *t*-test).
(b) Patients with dysthymia had earlier onset of illness ($P<0.001$, paired *t*-test), as well as a significantly earlier age of presentation.
(c) Surprisingly patients with dysthymia had a greater number of prior episodes which met DSM-III criteria for major depression ($P=0.004$, Fisher's exact test).

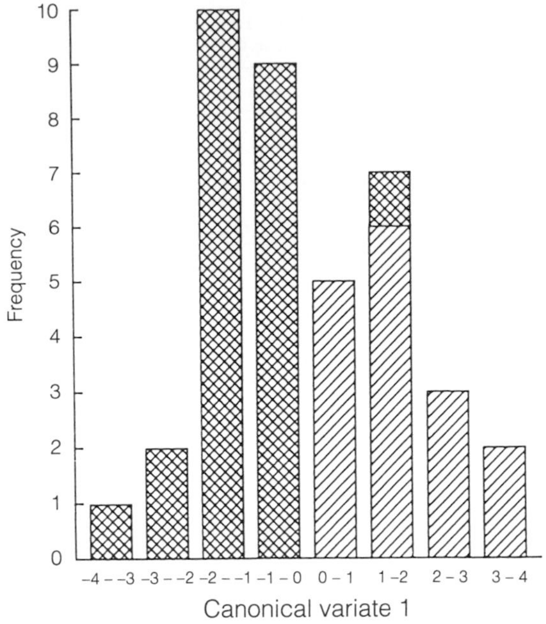

Fig. 4.1. Discriminant analysis: major affective episodes ▩ , *dysthymic grouping* ▨

(d) The family histories of the patients are given in Table 4.1. Patients with major affective episodes were more likely to have a first-degree relative with a past history of major affective illness ($P = 0.009$, Fisher's exact test). Although patients with dysthymia tended to have more relatives meeting DSM–III criteria for alcoholism, this difference did not reach statistical significance ($P = 0.11$, Fisher's exact test).

(e) Patients with dysthymia did not meet DSM–III criteria for personality disorder more frequently than did patients with major affective episodes. However, patients with dysthymia were more likely to have taken overdoses ($P = 0.01$, Fisher's exact test). Patients with dysthymia were more likely to have suffered separation from either parent before the age of 15 ($P = 0.002$) and particularly if this was due to parental divorce ($P < 0.001$, Fisher's exact test). Patients with dysthymia also had a smaller number of legitimate children ($P = 0.05$). Differences between the groups were not found for other variables measured.

A discriminant function analysis of all variables except the dysthymia score selected age of onset, HRSA score and number of experiences of separation before the age of 15 as the best discriminators between dysthymia and major affective episodes. Using these three items alone it was possible to identify correctly 96% of the patients with dysthymia and 94% of the patients with major affective episode.

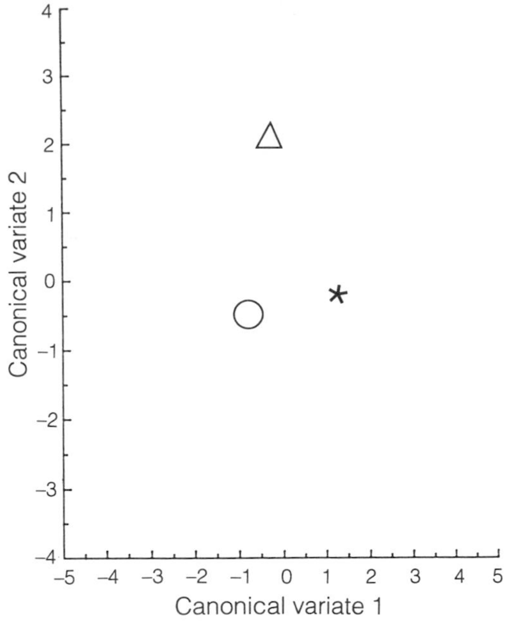

Fig. 4.2. Discriminant analysis for all depressives: means for major affective episode (★), dysthymic (○), other (△) grouping

The results of the discriminant analysis are given in Fig. 4.1, from which it can be seen that there is hardly any overlap between the patients with dysthymia and the patients with major affective illness. The separation between these groups is particularly clear in the case of canonical variate analysis (Fig. 4.2).

Subaffective dysthymic disorder compared with character spectrum disorder

Differences between SDD and CSD have been reported in terms of age at onset of illness, constancy of symptoms, personality characteristics, parental separation and divorce, and family history both of alcoholism and of affective illness (Rosenthal *et al*, 1981; Akiskal, 1983).

As shown in Table 4.2 no significant differences were found between patients with SDD and CSD in any of these variables. Among the variables listed above are a number of others which might reasonably have been thought to differentiate between the groups: none of them do so. As CSD has been considered to be a form of personality disorder it was thought that differences between CSD and SDD might be found for past history of truancy, number of public examinations passed, school-leaving age, longest

TABLE 4.2
Comparison of patients with SDD with those with CSD

	Subaffective dysthymic disorder (n = *15*)	*Character spectrum disorder* (n = *9*)	*Statistical significance*
Mean age at onset: years ± s.d.	16.0 (± 5.2)	18.3 (± 8.2)	NS
No. with DSM–III diagnosis of personality disorder	6	7	NS
Mean no. of experiences of separation before age of 15 (± s.d.)	1.1 (± 1.2)	1.1 (± 1.1)	NS
No. with family history of:			
alcoholism only	2	3	NS
affective disorder only	0	3	NS
alcoholism + affective disorder	1	5	NS
affective disorder + other illness	3	0	NS
Mean no. of affective episodes (± s.d.)	4.0 (± 2.6)	3.2 (± 4.1)	NS
Mean no. of hospital admissions (± s.d.)	1.9 (± 4.9)	1.5 (± 5.1)	NS
Mean no. of overdoses (± s.d.)	1.3 (± 2.1)	1.5 (± 3.9)	NS
Mean age when interviewed: years ± s.d.	34.2 (± 13.3)	29.7 (± 8.1)	NS
Sex ratio (females:males)	6:3	12:3	
Constancy of mood			
never have relief from symptoms	2	3	
sometimes have relief from symptoms	0	1	
often have relief from symptoms	7	11	

period of employment, longest period of unemployment, number of jobs, marital status, number of marriages, divorces and separations, number of criminal offences and number of patients with a criminal record: no differences between CSD and SDD were found for any of these variables.

All of the variables listed were entered into a discriminant function analysis: excluded from this list were those items such as Schneider's depressive typology which were used in the operational definition of SDD and CSD. The variables which best distinguished between SDD and CSD were the DSM–III criteria for recognising dysthymia and the number of past affective episodes. Using these two variables alone, 79% of the patients with CSD and 56% of the patients with SDD could be correctly identified.

No clear differences between the two populations could be demonstrated using canonical variance analysis (Fig. 4.3).

Discussion

This is the first report on patients meeting DSM–III criteria for dysthymia in an English centre. Over three months a psychiatric emergency service

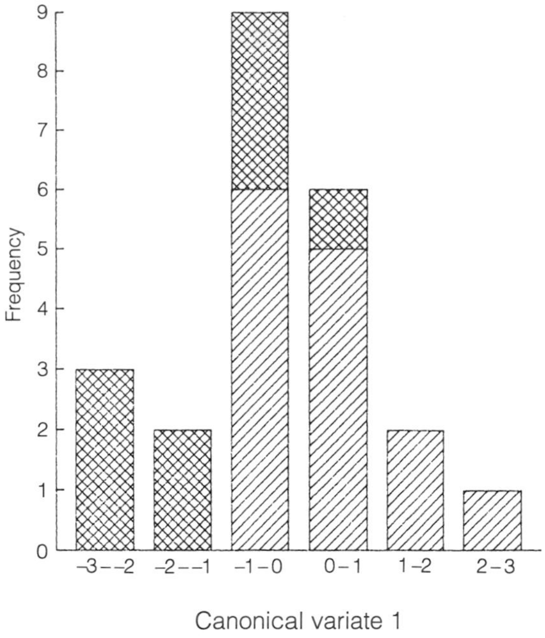

Fig. 4.3. Discriminant analysis for dysthymic patients: CHD ▨ , SUB ⊠ grouping without Schneider's score variables

in south London received 415 referrals, of whom 117 had never previously attended the hospital. Of these 117 patients 51 complained of depression, and 24 of these 51 depressives met DSM–III criteria for dysthymia. Not only did a high proportion (24/51) of people presenting meet the DSM–III criteria for dysthymia, they had also significantly more previous episodes of affective illness and more previous overdoses. Clearly the patients who meet DSM–III criteria for dysthymia present a significant clinical problem for the emergency service.

Lewis (1938) has argued against the subdivision of depressive disorders into subcategories. His view was that the heterogeneity of depression could be understood entirely in terms of severity and chronicity. Lewis would have argued that the only difference between patients with dysthymia and patients with major depression was that the dysthymics had milder but more chronic illnesses. Our findings argue against this view. The principal differences found in our study between dysthymia and major affective episode were age at onset, HRSA score and experiences of separation before the age of 15. Although age at onset is related to chronicity, neither of the other key variables is apparently related either to chronicity or to severity of depression: in particular the finding of higher anxiety scores in the less severely depressed group is opposed to Lewis' model. Instead our findings do support the validity of making a distinction between dysthymia and major affective episodes. Whether this clinical distinction can be supported by biological differences remains to be seen.

Our findings do not however support Akiskal's subdivision of dysthymia into the categories of SDD and CSD. Our sample size was slightly smaller than the one initially studied by Akiskal. Our sample was also qualitatively different in that Akiskal's sample included private patients and tertiary referrals whereas ours did not. However, none of the proposed discriminating factors between CSD and SDD even approached statistical significance.

Symposium discussion

DR HIRSCHFELD: Dr Murphy, I am a little unclear about the separation of the original population. Did the subjects who presented with dysthymia also meet criteria for major depression? If not, what brought them to an emergency service? Why would someone suffering from dysthymia be coming to an emergency service?

DR MURPHY: We had 24 dysthymics who presented to the emergency clinic whom we split in two separate ways. Firstly we split them into those who presented with double depression, a major affective episode imposed on a pre-existing dysthymic disorder. That took about 60% of our population. The other 40% were pure dysthymics, presenting in a chronic dysphoric state.

To make sure that their self-report of dysthymic criteria was not due to an autocognitive set because of their depressive illness, we contacted at least two family members or independent witnesses who were personally interviewed. The subjects are followed up for a minimum of two months, past the major depressive episode, so that they could then be reassigned to another grouping if they were no longer dysthymic. Within the dysthymic grouping, a split of double depression versus the pure dysthymics, we did exactly the same analyses, that is analyses of variance etc., and again there was no statistical difference between the groups at all, within the dysthymic grouping.

PROFESSOR AKISKAL: A point I would like to make to Dr Murphy is that it seems to me that in this very difficult area where symptomatologically we have great difficulty with separation, we should use some kind of biological measure. In Memphis we have used pharmacological dissection and sleep studies, which are the most robust in our study in terms of separation. Perhaps the results that led us to suggest subtypes are not yet sufficiently useful in terms of discrimination, but at least in the population that we studied the biological measures tended to distinguish the various subgroups quite well.

The other point I would like to make is along the lines of the one Dr Hirschfeld made earlier. An emergency clinic would not seem to be the best place to look at these patients, although a private practice would be fairly good.

I must say that among our core dysthymics many were physicians, lawyers and those kinds of people. In the long run we may have to add criteria which include profession. They seem to be quite different from other types of patients who are seen in more community settings who have a different kind of dysphoria. There is a great deal of human misery that manifests with mixtures of anxiety and depression and in different settings these may be different things. Clinically, separation is extremely difficult and subtyping should include something other than the usual clinical indices and personality indices and we should perhaps use as many biological measures as we can, to shed some light. I am actually quite pleased that in other studies, such as Dr Rihmer's (Chapter 10), especially with regard to biological measures, have actually replicated ours. The Association of Sleep Disorders Centers, in its recent classification, has endorsed that there is such a thing as a core group of dysthymics who have sleep abnormalities similar to those of major depressives.

I think the ultimate challenge for us is to be able to develop clinical criteria that are sufficiently selective. I think we are not yet there; Dr Seivewright and Dr Murphy (Chapter 3) have eloquently argued that clinical criteria, including those I have proposed, are still quite inadequate.

DR CHECKLEY (*chairman*): Dr Murphy and I would agree and we are doing a sleep study at the moment, but the data are not yet ready for presentation.

DR KELLER: I have a question for Dr Murphy about the past and the future. In terms of the variables you showed us, most of them were historical, so one question is on the reliability of those questions for people who come in with this type of dysphoric state. Have you done any reliability studies?

In terms of the future, you say you are concluding now that there are distinct entities, but have you followed the course to see whether there is any difference between the dysthymics and major depressives?

DR MURPHY: I will take your second question first, if I may. No, we have not done a follow-up to compare the course. With regard to your first question, concerning how reliable historians are, there is no absolute measure that we could use: that is why we always contacted at least two independent historians besides the patient, and they had to corroborate the evidence that the patient put forward, and if possible produce old psychiatric notes, where available.

DR QURESHI: I was interested to see the higher incidence of alcohol abuse in the families of the patients who came to your emergency clinic. Were they themselves abusing alcohol at the time, or was this not noted in the history?

Also, what possible significance is there in a history of increasing alcohol abuse in the family? I know that it is not statistically significant, but what pathway is mediating the dysthymia in that way?

DR MURPHY: I cannot begin to answer the second part of your question because we found no difference between the families with regard to alcohol. With regard to the first part of your question, yes, some people were abusing alcohol but not with significant differences between any of the groupings. It was a small proportion who were abusing alcohol and it did not reach statistical significance. They were not alcoholic.

DR SEIVEWRIGHT: I was moderately surprised when looking at our data to find no incidence of alcohol abuse or dependence in our follow-up diagnoses. The criteria for alcohol abuse in DSM–III are not very demanding and yet we did not encounter it in our sample.

PROFESSOR HAMILTON: I am afraid I do not know very much about dysthymic disorders as such, but for many years I have been looking into what used to be called, and I hope still is, the prodromal symptoms of acute depressive illness. My attention was first drawn to this in 1956 and later on there was a paper by Peter Hays (1964), which I am always quoting about this prodromal period, showing that before the development of an acute depressive illness there was a period in which a patient might show either depressive symptoms or anxiety symptoms. From my own experience, the anxiety symptoms looked like pure anxiety neurosis.

One of the things I looked at is whether patients do have this prodromal period or not and how long the prodromal period is. Not surprisingly, I discovered that with those who have prodromal periods, the frequency distribution of the length of this period is a log normal distribution, as almost everything in the affective disorders is. This would probably indicate why the search for pure dysthymic disorder is so difficult. There are obviously many more patients who have a short period than those who have a long period. The long periods which apparently extend for most of the lifetime will be extremely rare.

DR CHECKLEY (*chairman*): Is there anyone with data to comment on the distribution of the length of dysthymia? Is there any bimodality there?

DR KELLER: I am not sure whether this quite gets at your comment, but we find that among the people who have had at least two years of chronic low-grade symptoms, the median duration is between six and eight years. So once they hit the two-year point it is rather extended. In our study, the median duration of illness of people who have had a major depressive episode is about six months in which there was no underlying low-grade or prodromal depression. Only about 15% or 25% of the people with major depression had been ill for less than two months before they came into the study. It turned out that duration of illness for the major depressives without dysthymia is the clinical variable most strongly predictive of recovery. Chronology of illness is a critical factor in predicting course and although ours is not a treatment study, it presumably predicts treatment response as well.

References

AKISKAL, H. (1983) Dysthymic disorder: psychopathology of proposed chronic depressive subtypes. *American Journal of Psychiatry*, **140**, 11–20.

——, BITAR, A. H., PUZANTIAN, V. R., *et al* (1978) The nosological status of neurotic depression: a prospective 3–4 year follow-up examination in the light of the primary–secondary and the unipolar–bipolar dichotomies. *Archives of General Psychiatry*, **35**, 756–766.

——, ROSENTHAL, T., RADWAN, F., *et al* (1980) Clinical and sleep EEG findings separating subaffective dysthymias from character spectrum disorders. *Archives of General Psychiatry*, **37**, 777–783.

——, KING, O., ROSENTHAL, T., *et al* (1981) Chronic depressions, Part I. Clinical and familial characteristics in 135 probands. *Journal of Affective Disorders*, **3**, 297–315.

AMERICAN PSYCHIATRIC ASSOCIATION (1980) *Diagnostic and Statistical Manual of Mental Disorders* (3rd edn) (DSM–III). Washington, DC: APA.

FEIGHNER, J. P., ROBINS, E., GUZE, S. B., *et al* (1972) Diagnostic criteria for use in psychiatric research. *Archives of General Psychiatry*, **26**, 57–63.

HAMILTON, M. (1959) The assessment of anxiety state by ratings. *British Journal of Medical Psychology*, **32**, 50–55.

—— (1960) A rating scale for depression. *Journal of Neurology, Neurosurgery and Psychiatry*, **23**, 56–62.

HAYS, P. (1964) Modes of onset of psychotic depression. *British Medical Journal*, *ii*, 779–784.

LEWIS, A. J. (1938) States of depression: their clinical and aetiological differentiation. *British Medical Journal*, *ii*, 875–878.

ROSENTHAL, T. L., AKISKAL, H. S., SCOTT-STRAUSS, A., *et al* (1981) Familial and developmental factors in charactological depressions. *Journal of Affective Disorders*, 183–192.

SCHNEIDER, K. (1958) *Psychopathic Personalities* (trans. M. W. Hamilton). London: Cassell.

5 Depression and dysphoria in old age

C. L. E. KATONA and G. T. BELL

The high frequency and disabling nature of depressive symptoms in old age present major clinical challenges in both diagnosis and management. Recent epidemiological studies have benefited from better sampling procedures, the use of operational definitions and the availability of more appropriate research instruments. These, in turn, have allowed clearer identification of a significant group of patients in whom depressive symptoms do not fulfil the criteria for major depressive episode (MDE). The term 'senile dysphoria' has been applied to this group of patients, in whom certain social and personality characteristics have also been identified.

This chapter reviews the epidemiological evidence for the use of such a concept and its relationship to major depressive disorder in terms of clinical correlates and natural history.

Epidemiology: methodological problems

Estimates of the prevalence of depression in the elderly vary widely (Post & Shulman, 1985). Hospital-based studies have, in general, reported a lower prevalence of depression in the elderly than in the general population, while many community-based studies have suggested the reverse. Such discrepancies result from a number of methodological problems that have only recently been adequately addressed.

The first of these problems is in the selection of subjects to be studied. This area is well reviewed by Kay & Bergmann (1980), who emphasised that hospital-based samples are particularly highly selected and unrepresentative. They regard tracing a community cohort over time as the ideal method, although seldom practicable; most studies have adopted a 'census' approach, studying a defined population over a short period. The proportion of subjects refusing to participate in such studies is variable and, if high, may result in bias in the sample actually examined. Most community samples use data collected by lay interviewers, who may not have adequate

TABLE 5.1
Depression rating scales in old age

Criteria characteristic of depression in the elderly	*HRSD*	*IPSCE*	*Zung*	*Beck*	*CES-D*	*GDS*	*WKFD*	*CARE*	*DSM-III*
Decreased capacity to care for oneself	x								
Guilt	x			x		x		x	x
Change of appetite		x	x	x	x			x	x
Loss of self-esteem		x	x	x	x				x
Decreased sense of life-long accomplishments				x		x		x	
Emptiness			x			x			
Locus of control (helplessness)						x			
History of depressive feelings								x	
Envy						x			
Critical of others		x							
Hypochondriasis	x							x	
Somatic complaints	x	x	x						
Perceived cognitive deficit		x	x			x		x	x

HRSD = Hamilton Rating Scale for Depression; IPSCE = Inventory of Psychic and Somatic Complaints of the Elderly; Zung = Zung Self-Rating Depression Scale; Beck = Beck Depression Inventory; CES-D = Center for Epidemiologic Studies Depression Scale; GDS = Geriatric Depression Scale; WKFD = Wakefield Depression Inventory; CARE = Comprehensive Assessment and Referral Evaluation Schedule.

training in distinguishing significant depressive symptoms from the physical problems and dissatisfactions often experienced by elderly people. Freedman *et al* (1982) suggest family practitioner consultation as an appropriate point for making accurate estimates of depression in the elderly, because of the family practitioner's role in the care of the individual's physical and psychological well-being.

The second problem is that of defining and detecting depression within the population being studied. Copeland (1981) has made a valuable contribution to our understanding of the concept of a psychiatric 'case', particularly in relation to the question of intervention. Criteria for individual symptoms need to be operationalised, and the interview techniques for detecting them standardised, as preliminaries to the rigorous definition of the criteria for 'caseness'.

The third problem relates to the selection of instruments for detecting cases. The most widely used techniques are questionnaires, semistructured interviews and unstructured psychiatric interviews. The elderly have particular difficulties in reading, understanding and responding appropriately to questionnaires and the results of interviews may be influenced considerably by the training and personality of the interviewer. The high prevalence of both acute and chronic physical illness among the elderly can make the distinction between physical and psychiatric symptoms difficult, even for the experienced interviewer. Table 5.1 (adapted and expanded from Weiss *et al* (1986)) shows that although commonly used rating scales for depression are sufficient to generate DSM–III diagnoses (American Psychiatric Association, 1980), they do not, for the most part, address the symptoms most characteristic of depression in old age. It is clearly necessary to ensure that measures used in the study of depression in the elderly are both valid and reliable in the specific population being examined.

This is, in turn, relates to the fourth methodological problem: the clinical presentation of depression in old age. Many elderly subjects complain of hypochondriacal symptoms or sleep disturbance rather than depressed mood. The effect of this can be minimised by the inclusion of a separate 'somatic symptoms' rating scale, as incorporated in the diagnostic schedule of Copeland *et al* (1986). Good *et al* (1987) used a varimax factor analysis to demonstrate four factor groupings which have clinical relevance in the depressed elderly: depression, anxiety, cognitive impairment, and psychosomatic disorder. High scores on the depression factor were observed to be frequently associated with high scores on the psychosomatic disorder factor, confirming other findings of the importance of somatic symptoms in depression in the elderly. Gurland (1976) also showed an increase in somatic concern in the elderly depressed. The clinical distinction between depression and dementia may be a further problem (Katona & Aldridge, 1985). Although the syndrome of depressive pseudodementia, in which cognitive dysfunction is a prominent feature of a depressive illness in old age, is well recognised (Bulbena & Berrios, 1986), it is likely that many such patients turn out on follow-up to have dementing illnesses; Kral (1983) found this to be the case in 20 of 22 subjects. The danger of demented subjects contaminating a survey sample of elderly depressives is thus considerable.

Freedman *et al* (1982) stress the need for a new conceptualisation of depressive syndromes in the elderly as well as new methods of evaluation to permit detection of cases of depressive disorder that may go unrecognised at present, and to distinguish complaints of sadness or other types of emotional and physical pain from depression.

The concept of dysphoria

One of the essential features of depressive illness is 'dysphoria'—"a state of unease or discomfort" (*Concise Oxford Dictionary*). Dysphoric mood is central to the DSM–III criteria both for MDE, in which a minimum of four core depressive symptoms lasting at least two weeks are also required, and for 'dysthymic disorder' (or depressive neurosis), in which dysphoric mood and a minimum of three core depressive symptoms must have been present for at least two years. A number of studies in the elderly have examined (a) dysphoric mood, (b) MDE, and (c) dysthymic disorder; others have used non-DSM–III descriptions which fit more or less well into these broad categories.

Only a small minority of the studies reviewed in this chapter make specific contributions to the problem of case definition. The studies by Copeland *et al* (1987*a*,*b*), using a computerised diagnostic package, AGECAT, differentiated between subcases, in which minor mood symptoms and some symptoms of non-specific depression were evident, and cases of either depressive neurosis or psychosis. Gillis & Zabow (1982) defined dysphoria as a score of less than 15 on both the Life Satisfaction Index (indicating poor life satisfaction) (Neugarten *et al*, 1961) and the Hamilton Rating Scale for Depression (Hamilton, 1960) (indicating only relatively mild depressive symptoms). A study by Blazer & Williams (1980) used the term 'dysphoria' for individuals with four or more dysphoric symptoms but having less than four of the DSM–III criteria for MDE as rated in the Duke–OARS Multidimensional Functional Assessment Questionnaire.

The applicability of the concept of dysthymia, as used elsewhere in this volume, to an elderly population has been reviewed by Moore (1985). The groups identified by Gillis & Zabow (1982) appear to be those most closely resembling Akiskal's (1983) character spectrum dysthymia, whereas the high association of dysphoric mood with physical impairment reported by Blazer & Williams (1980) suggests a subgroup corresponding roughly to Akiskal's (1983) secondary dysthymia. The dysphoric elderly are clearly a heterogeneous group. Further work is needed to assess the applicability of Akiskal's classification in the elderly.

Epidemiological studies

Estimates for the prevalence of depression in elderly subjects vary widely (Table 5.2). This variability may, as has been discussed above, be explained by a number of factors. Kay & Bergmann (1980) have reviewed several early studies that relied mainly on open-ended clinical interviews and on short symptom questionnaires. The main conclusion to emerge from these studies is that with increasing age, depression becomes the most prevalent neurosis although psychotic affective illness in old age is relatively rare. Bergmann (1971), in a study of neuroses of old age, showed that while anxiety was the most common disorder in the 'chronic' neurotic group, depression was far commoner among 'late-onset' neurotics. These studies confirm the findings of the classic study by Kay *et al* (1964) in which mild degrees of 'affective disorders and neuroses' were found in 16.2% and moderate to severe such disorders in 10%. It proved impossible to distinguish accurately between endogenous and reactive depressions but the prevalence of endogenous affective disorder was estimated at 1.3–3%, depending whether past psychiatric history was taken into account. The findings of an important study of volunteers by Gianturco & Busse (1978) are similar. They studied 264 volunteers aged 60 and over who were willing to complete interviews and clinical examinations lasting two days as part of a longitudinal study

TABLE 5.2
Epidemiological studies of depression in old age

Type of study	*Rating*	*% male*	*% female*	*% total*
Rating scale				
Raymond *et al* (1980)	WKFD	—	—	34.5
Murrell *et al* (1983)	CES-D	14	19	17.5
Lalive D'Epinay (1985)	Wang	23	34	28
Kivela *et al* (1986)	Zung	7	—	—
Ben-Arie *et al* (1987)	PSE	—	—	16.5
Griffiths *et al* (1987)	HRSD	1	15	8
Morgan *et al* (1987)	SAD	—	—	9.8
Diagnostic systems				
Blazer & Williams (1980)	OARS + DSM-III	13	16	15
Myers *et al* (1984)	DIS	1.2	3.7	2.7
Hasegawa (1985)	ICD-9	—	—	0.9
Kay *et al* (1985)	AGECAT	—	—	14.2
Copeland *et al* (1987*a*)	AGECAT	7.6	13.6	11.3
Copeland *et al* (1987*b*)	AGECAT	13	20	18
Special settings				
Cheah & Beard (1980)	Clinical	—	—	7
Gillis & Zabow (1982)	HDRS/LSI	14	9	10
MacDonald & Dunn (1982)	CARE	—	—	19.1
Mann *et al* (1984)	CARE	—	—	38
Borson *et al* (1986)	Zung	24	—	—
MacDonald (1986)	CARE	19.3	36.8	30.6

of ageing. Although they attempted to make their sample demographically representative of the local population in Durham, North Carolina, the sample may well have been biased by the self-selection of volunteers for such detailed interviews. No information is given as to method for assessing depression, but 21% of subjects were recorded as depressed.

Rating-scale studies

Several of these studies rely entirely on data from rating scales. Raymond *et al* (1980), using the Wakefield scale (Snaith *et al*, 1971) which does not include any of the depressive features particularly associated with old age depression, found a prevalence of significant depressive symptoms in 34.5% of a randomly selected community sample, with a refusal rate of only 12.5%. Murrell *et al* (1983) used the Center for Epidemiologic Studies Depression Scale (CES-D) (Refleff, 1977) in a total sample of 2517 subjects aged 55 and over. The rating used contains 20 items and the chosen cut-off score identifies 70% of clinically defined depressed subjects and only 14% of a previously tested community sample. Laudably, they present their data stratified in age bands and report an overall prevalence of depression of

17.5% in their subsample aged 65 and over. Their overall response rate was 80%. Kivela *et al* (1986) reported a follow-up study of a sample of Finnish men previously examined in middle age. It is unclear how representative the initial sample was but 93% of survivors were available to follow-up and, using the Zung Self-Rating Depression Scale (Zung, 1965) with a cut-off of 60 points or over, a prevalence of depression of 7% was found. The authors note that decreased libido, diurnal variation in mood, emptiness, and personal devaluation were the most commonly reported symptoms. A stratified random sample of elderly Swiss subjects by Lalive D'Epinay (1985) used the Wang Depression Scale (Wang, 1975). No information is given as to the criteria used for defining depressed subjects but 28% overall scored 'high' on the scale. Griffiths *et al* (1987) sought volunteers among a sample of 1500 mobile elderly subjects identified from general practice registers. They used a structured interview to elicit the symptoms listed in the Hamilton Rating Scale for Depression and, with a cut-off of 13 points to identify depression, reported an overall prevalence of 8%. This result is difficult to interpret since, as the authors themselves point out, the scale they use is intended specifically for measuring severity of depression in a sample already diagnosed clinically as suffering from a depressive illness. Morgan *et al* (1987) surveyed a stratified sample of elderly subjects in Nottingham using the Symptoms of Anxiety and Depression scale (SAD; Bedford *et al*, 1976). They found a prevalence of depression of 9.8% using the criteria of a total SAD score greater than 6 and a depression subscale of 4 or more. These criteria for depression agreed poorly with clinical ratings in a small subsample. A more conservative cut-off (total SAD 7/8 and a depressive subscale score >6) maximised agreement with clinical judgement, and gave a prevalence for depression of 4.9%. Ben-Arie *et al* (1987) examined a random community sample of 139 coloured persons aged 65 and over in Capetown, South Africa. They used the Present State Examination (PSE; Wing *et al*, 1974) as their standard interview schedule and excluded demented subjects using the Mini-Mental State Examination of Folstein *et al* (1975). Having excluded subjects with significant cognitive impairment and with diagnoses other than depression, they found that 23 subjects (16.5%) had sufficient depressive symptoms to enable a tentative PSE/CATEGO computer diagnosis of depression to be made. Full psychiatric interviewing of these subjects confirmed the diagnosis of depression in 19, giving a prevalence rate of clinically confirmed depression of 13.7%. Six subjects had 'threshold' levels of depression and 13 definite depression. The most common depressive symptoms and signs were depressed mood, observed depression, morning depression and early waking. Irritability, nervous tension, tension pains, and worrying were also commonly reported by depressed subjects, although guilt was absent.

It is clear that prevalence rates from rating-scale data vary widely despite considerable care being given to ensure that samples examined are representative. A number of studies attempt to reach beyond the limitation of rating scales by using standardised diagnostic systems.

Diagnostic system studies

Several more recent studies are summarised in Table 5.2.

Blazer & Williams (1980) carried out detailed standardised questionnaires on 997 subjects (85% of the total sample approached) in Durham, North Carolina. They extracted seven items from the questionnaire enabling an assessment of dysphoric mood to be made and a further 11 items allowing a DSM–III diagnosis of major depressive illness to be made or excluded. Of the 14.7% of subjects who showed dysphoric mood, 3.7% fulfilled criteria for major depressive episode. Half of the latter group had depressive illness secondary to cognitive dysfunction or thought disorder. Kay *et al* (1985) examined a random sample of elderly subjects in Hobart, Tasmania, using the Geriatric Mental State interview (GMS) to generate both AGECAT and DSM–III diagnoses. They report moderate to severe depression on the AGECAT system in 14.2% of subjects and DSM–III major depression in 10.2%. They comment that their DSM–III prevalence rate is higher than that of most comparable studies but provide little explanation for this, although stressing that the symptoms of poor sleep, reduced energy, etc., that are crucial to DSM–III diagnosis, are reported very frequently in their sample, whereas thoughts of guilt and suicide are relatively rare. Also, their sample was restricted to subjects aged 70 and over. Copeland *et al* (1987*b*) used the same diagnostic system as Kay *et al* (1985) and report an AGECAT prevalence of 16.2% in a New York sample of 445 subjects aged 65 and over, and 19.5% in a London sample of 396 subjects. Prevalences for depressive psychosis were 1.85% and 3.3% respectively. DSM–III diagnoses were also available for the London sample, 4.6% having major affective disorder and an additional 1.8% suffering from bereavement reactions. A further study by Copeland *et al* (1987*a*) of 1070 subjects in Liverpool reported a prevalence of depressive illness of 11.3%, 2.9% with psychotic features. Myers *et al* (1984), in a major study of the prevalence of psychiatric disorder in over 9000 adults, found that in their subsample aged 65 and over the overall prevalence of affective disorder of any kind (using DSM–III criteria) was 2.7%, and that of major depressive episode was 1%. Hasegawa (1985) reviews three large-scale studies in Japan all using ICD–9 clinical diagnoses and reporting prevalence of depressive illness of 1–2%.

It is clear that there is considerable discrepancy between the high prevalence of depressive symptoms on the one hand, and depressive illness sufficient to fulfil DSM–III or ICD–9 criteria (World Health Organization, 1978) on the other. Some of the studies previously cited have addressed this crucial issue by subdividing subjects showing depressive symptoms into diagnostic groupings (Table 5.3). Blazer & Williams (1980) further analysed the 11% of their sample who while showing significantly dysphoric mood did not fulfil DSM–III criteria for major depressive episode. Of the 110 subjects, 45 exhibited a pure syndrome of dysphoric mood and 65 showed dysphoric mood in the setting of significant physical illness. Kay *et al* (1985)

TABLE 5.3
Epidemiology of dysthymia/dysphoria in old age

Study	*% male*	*% female*	*% total*
Blazer & Williams (1980)	4.3	5.9	4.5 Dysphoria
Gillis & Zabow (1982)	37	13	17 Dysphoria
Myers *et al* (1984)	1	2	1.5 DSM–III dysthymia
Kay *et al* (1985)	—	—	19 Dysphoric mood
Borson *et al* (1986)	14	—	— Depressed not MDE
Copeland *et al* (1987*b*)	—	—	6.3 DSM–III dysthymia

using the same DSM–III diagnostic criteria as Blazer & Williams (1980) found that 19% of their subjects fulfilled criteria for dysphoric mood but not for MDE. They comment that this large subsample "must include dysthymia disorder proper". Unfortunately they do not present data on how many subjects fulfil DSM–III criteria for dysthymia. Two recent studies have however estimated the prevalence of DSM–III dysthymia in an elderly population. Myers *et al* (1984) in a study of six-month prevalence of psychiatric illness found that 1.5% of their elderly sample fulfilled DSM–III criteria for dysthymia. Their interview schedules did not however include information on current duration of symptoms and their dysthymia figures refer to dysthymia at any time in the individual's life rather than in the immediate past two years. Copeland *et al* (1987*b*) found a prevalence of DSM–III dysthymia of 6.3% in their London sample. Although objective confirmation of duration of illness was not available, all subjects diagnosed as dysthymic provided self-reports of duration of illness exceeding two years.

It seems clear that depressive symptoms are common in the elderly and that several of the conventional measures for rating depression produce relatively high scores in an elderly population, at least in part because of the problems of fatigue, changes in sleep pattern, and increasing physical ill health associated with normal ageing. Those few studies that have adopted more rigorous criteria for defining depressive subsyndromes show that some elderly patients with depressive symptoms fulfil criteria for dysthymia but that, particularly when the chronicity criterion is applied rigorously, there remains a considerable population of subjects who have clearly dysphoric mood but cannot be classified within DSM–III as having either major depressive episode or dysthymic disorder. These subjects, many of whom fulfil AGECAT criteria for depressive syndrome, should, in the view of the results of Copeland *et al* (1987*a*), be seen as suffering from depressive neurosis.

Special settings

A number of studies have estimated the prevalence of depression in elderly people in specific settings. In a study of white residents of old-age homes in Cape Town, Gillis & Zabow (1982) found that in a sample of 300 elderly white residents, 16.6% exhibited dysphoria and 10% showed similar levels of poor life satisfaction, but had a Hamilton score of greater than 15, indicating at least moderate depression. MacDonald & Dunn (1982) studied residents in old people's homes and elderly in-patients and day patients at psychiatric hospitals. Of the 633 subjects in the sample, depression ratings could be performed on 397, and a prevalence of 19.1% was reported using the depression subscale of the Brief Assessment Schedule (BAS), part of the CARE interview which itself is an adaptation of the GMS interview used by Copeland *et al* (1986). Mann *et al* (1984) used the same rating instrument in a survey of all residents of old people's homes in Camden, London. They were able to interview 82% of the total population of 535 subjects. One-third were severely demented, and of the 289 subjects in whom depression ratings were obtainable 38% showed significant depressive symptoms. Interestingly the early study of Kay *et al* (1964) reported an extremely low incidence of affective illness and neurosis in the institutionalised elderly. This most likely represents differences in admission practices to such residential care over the past 20 years.

Borson *et al* (1986) examined 917 elderly male medical out-patients (aged 60 and over) using the Zung scale to estimate prevalence of depression. Only 44% of the original sample completed the Zung questionnaire and of those, 24% had significant depressive symptoms (total Zung score greater than or equal to 60). Borson *et al* estimate that this represents a prevalence of major depression of 10% on the basis of extrapolations from other samples using the Zung scale. The remainder of their Zung-positive sample (14%), although exhibiting significant depressive symptoms, did not fulfil DSM-III criteria for MDE. These subjects might appropriately be described as dysphoric. It is not however clear from their paper whether such extrapolation is equally valid for an adult and an elderly population. Cheah and colleagues (Cheah *et al*, 1979; Cheah & Beard, 1980) studied 262 elderly medical in-patients, each of whom received a clinical interview from a "geropsychiatrist" attached to the medical team. A total of 31.3% were reported to show features of "depression/dysphoria". The great majority of these cases were mild, indicating a duration of less than two weeks and a global degree of disability due to depression of 20% or less. Only 7% showed moderate or severe "depression/dysphoria" and no details are given as to the symptoms associated with these diagnoses.

An interesting study by MacDonald (1986) examined a random sample of elderly general practice attenders, using the same interview schedule as MacDonald & Dunn (1982) and Mann *et al* (1984). Only 10% of the total sample of 235 subjects refused to be interviewed, and a prevalence of depression of 30.6% was reported using slightly more stringent severity criteria than the other studies using the CARE interview in order to achieve the best agreement with diagnoses based on full clinical interviewing. It seems clear that both elderly subjects in residential settings and those attending their general practitioners show rates of significant depressive symptoms somewhat higher than those reported from community samples.

It is unfortunate that none of the cited studies (except Borson *et al* (1986)) provided a breakdown of their depressed subjects into diagnostic categories on DSM–III or any other external diagnostic system.

Correlates of depression and dysphoria in old age

Several epidemiological studies have examined sociodemographic, biological and personality correlates of depression in old age. Such associations with dysphoria and dysthymia in the elderly have received much less attention.

The great majority of studies indicate that depression in the elderly is commoner in women. Among rating-scale studies, significantly higher proportions of depressed 'cases' in women are reported by Murrell *et al* (1983), Raymond *et al* (1980), Good *et al* (1987) and Lalive D'Epinay (1985). Studies using diagnostic criteria show the same trend but to a less marked and less consistent degree. Although MacDonald (1986) found that 36.8% of elderly women and only 19.3% of elderly men fulfilled CARE criteria for depression, Blazer & Williams (1980) found that only a very small non-significant excess of women fulfilled DSM–III criteria for depression. Similarly Myers *et al* (1984) found no significant difference in six-month prevalence of major depression in men and women aged over 65. Kay *et al* (1964) using Roth's (1955) classification found that severe affective disorders and neurosis were present in 12.2% of elderly women against 8.8% of men, and Gillis & Zabow (1982) in a South African population found a marked excess of depression in men. Copeland *et al* (1987*b*) found, in both their New York and London samples, that 50% more elderly women than men overall fulfilled AGECAT criteria for depression but that this trend was reversed in the very old, with a marked excess of depressed men aged over 85. Copeland *et al* further reported that within very elderly women there was a significant reduction in prevalence of depression with increasing old age and that this trend was not apparent in men.

The relationship between sex and dysphoria/dysthymia is less clear. Kay *et al* (1964) found that among their mild affective disorders and neuroses, the prevalence in women was 20.6% and in men only 8.7%. Bergmann (1971) reports depressive neuroses in 11% of elderly women and only 4% of men. Myers *et al* (1984) however report only a non-significant trend towards higher prevalence of dysthymia in women, and no significant difference in prevalence of dysphoria by sex is reported by Blazer & Williams (1980).

Several other studies have examined the relationship between depression and age within an elderly population. Good *et al* (1987) found a significant ($P<0.01$) relationship between increasing age and depression, and Kay *et al* (1985) found that DSM–III major depressive episode was present in only 6.3% of those aged 70–80 and 15.5% of those aged 80 and over. The relationship between minor depressive illness and age is less clear. Blazer

& Williams (1980) found a trend significant at the 10% level for dysphoria to be more frequent in the 65–74 age group whereas Kay *et al* (1985) found dysphoria to be present in 22.4% of those subjects aged 80 and over and only 16.5% of those aged 70–79.

Physical health is frequently reported to correlate with depression in the elderly. Murrell *et al* (1983) found a significant ($P<0.001$) relationship between subjectively reported general ill health and CES–D scores. In an important study of severe depression in old age using the PSE, Murphy (1982) found that 39% of her depressed subjects and only 26% of controls had significant physical health problems. Raymond *et al* (1980) found that subjective complaints of ill health were present in a high proportion of depressed subjects and that this accounted for 28% of the variance between depressed and normal subjects. The association between specific physical problems and depression has received less attention. Mann *et al* (1984) in a sample from an old people's home found a significant excess of urinary incontinence and visual problems in depressed subjects.

Physical illness appears to be an important correlate of dysphoria as well. In their review, Kay & Bergmann (1980) found physical illness to be frequently present in neurotic elderly men, and Blazer & Williams (1980) found that 6.5% of their elderly subjects showed dysphoria in association with physical ill health. Gillis & Zabow (1982) reported a significant increase in current physical illness and handicaps in the dysphorics (28%) compared with the depressed (3%) or the controls (10%).

Genetic factors are generally reported (Mendlewicz, 1976) to be less apparent in elderly depressives than in their younger counterparts. A number of specific biological variables do however appear to be associated with the depressions of old age. Salzman (1985) reviewed a number of studies of the dexamethasone suppression test (DST) in elderly depressed subjects and concluded that although in normal ageing there is no change in the extent to which endogenous cortisol production escapes early from suppression by dexamethasone, such early escape is more frequently seen in elderly than in younger depressed subjects. He concluded that DST non-suppression has a particularly high specificity for depression in old age. An important study by Jacoby & Levy (1980) of computerised tomography in normal, depressed, and demented elderly subjects found that although there was no overall difference between depressed and control subjects, there was an important subgroup of elderly depressives showing marked ventricular enlargement.

Social correlates of depression have also been examined in some detail. Murrell *et al* (1983) reported an increased rate of depression in elderly subjects on low incomes although no such relationship with DSM–III MDE was found by Blazer & Williams (1980). Two British studies (Murphy, 1982; Dallosso *et al*, 1986) found significant excesses of depression in elderly subjects of low social class. Mann *et al* (1984) reported increased prevalence of depression in residents of old people's homes from minority religious groupings (Roman Catholic, Jewish, non-conformist). Murrell *et al* (1983) found a significantly higher rate of depression in rural than urban dwellers. A similar result was reported Lalive D'Epinay (1985). She found that the excess of depression that she reported in elderly women was restricted to retired rural farm workers and urban blue-collar workers. She concluded that depression in elderly women is a reflection of 'culture shock'.

Several studies report a relationship between marital status and depression. The separated and divorced (Murrell *et al*, 1983; Borson *et al*, 1986) and the widowed (Blazer & Williams, 1980; Murrell *et al*, 1983) exhibit more depressive illness than married or single subjects. A more general relationship with social isolation was reported by Morgan *et al* (1987) who found a significant relationship between depressive symptoms and low rates of social engagement, and by Raymond *et al* (1980) who found depression frequently associated with being housebound. A similar relationship was reported by Hale (1982) to be present in elderly women but not men. Reduced activity in depressed elderly subjects has also been reported in both sexes (Griffiths *et al*, 1987) and in men only (Hale, 1982), although whether this is reflecting cause or effect is unclear. Murphy (1982) found that 42% of her depressed subjects and only 19% of controls had experienced recent major social difficulties.

The specific experience of loss events has received most attention. Murphy (1982) found that 48% of depressed subjects and only 23% of controls had experienced major life events and Linn *et al* (1980) found that arguments with relatives, accidents and bereavements were significantly more frequently reported by depressed subjects. Recent financial loss was found more frequently in depressed subjects by Hale *et al* (1982) and by MacDonald (1986).

As with biological variables, the social correlates of dysphoria and dysthymia in old age have received scant attention. Gillis & Zabow (1982) found their dysphoric subjects to show marked present social isolation as well as reduced rates of social contact in the past. Blazer & Williams (1980) reported a trend towards increased poverty in dysphoric subjects and a non-significant trend for dysphoria to be commoner in widowed, separated and divorced subjects.

Surprisingly, few recent studies have examined personality variables in old age depression. Post & Shulman (1985) commented on the difficulty in defining personality in retrospect. In a long-term follow-up study Ciompi (1969) reported that subjects whose pre-morbid personality had earlier been described as "anal-obsessional-meticulous" or as "oral-overdependent-hysteriform" were more likely to have poor outcomes, whereas subjects formerly described as "impulsive-irritable-emotive" tended to have better outcomes.

The situation regarding dysphoria is marginally clearer. Blazer & Williams (1980) found that alcohol abuse, use of analgesics and a perceived need for treatment for 'nerves' were significantly commoner in elderly dysphorics than in the normal elderly, and concluded that dysphoria in old age is a reflection of "decreased life satisfaction and periodic grief secondary to the physical, social, and economic difficulties encountered by ageing individuals in the community''. Gillis & Zabow (1982) found that dysphoric subjects exhibited ''life long manifestations of undue dependency, poor coping behaviour and inadequacy in inter-personal relationships'' on the basis of a close inquiry as to past personality from relatives, friends, and carers of their elderly subjects. They concluded that elderly dysphorics ''become increasingly like themselves''. Post & Shulman (1985), notwithstanding their misgivings about retrospective assessments of personality, emphasised the importance of ''innate and long standing personality factors'' in the aetiology of dysphoria.

In conclusion it seems clear that a number of biological and social factors, notably female sex, DST non-suppression, social isolation, and loss events are frequently associated with the development of moderate to severe depression and may be of aetiological importance. Minor depression appears to be more closely related to physical illness and to long-standing personality factors. It is clear that the role of social and biological factors in the minor depressions of old age merits much closer attention in future studies.

The natural history of depression in old age

There have been surprisingly few 'naturalistic' follow-up studies of depressive subjects in which the results have not been significantly distorted by initial entry criteria. Relevant studies can conveniently be divided into those of depression into old age and of depression starting in old age.

Depression into old age

Long-term follow-up information on hospital samples is provided by Angst (1981) and by Ciompi (1969). The samples are of subjects whose illnesses began before the age of 65 and where follow-up has occurred into old age. Angst (1981) reported on the onset, course and outcome of 406 patients with affective disorders admitted to the Burgholzli Hospital in Zurich between 1959 and 1963 and who were studied prospectively at five-year intervals until 1980. Thirty-seven per cent of unipolar depressives and 15% of those with bipolar illnesses had no relapses during the 20-year follow-up. Unipolar subjects with early onset of illness and bipolar subjects had a relapse rate of about 25% after the age of 65, whereas late-onset unipolars had a relapse rate of over 40% until age 74, which then fell to 25%. Angst emphasised that none of his subjects received lithium prophylaxis, but the use of other drugs or electroconvulsive therapy (ECT) was not specified and no information was given on other prognostic features or on mortality rate.

Ciompi's (1969) study from Lausanne consisted of a follow-up of all patients admitted to the University Psychiatric Hospital aged less than 65 and followed up to 1963 when they were aged between 66 and 90 and had been followed up for 1–52 years. A total of 555 subjects had been admitted with depressive illnesses and 97% were retraced. The average duration of follow-up was 20.5 years. It was concluded that depressive symptoms became gradually less severe in the majority of patients, one-third of whom had no relapse after the age of 65 and another third had less frequent and less severe episodes in old age than previously. One-third, however, exhibited chronic depressive symptoms in old age and there was a tendency for somatised depressive symptoms to replace self-accusatory depressive ideas. Even in those subjects with relatively good outcomes, chronic minor affective symptoms were commonplace. "More than half of our former depressed patients showed, in senescence, symptoms such as general dissatisfaction, despair, mistrust, demanding behaviour, hypochondria and anxiety". This was associated with decreases in vitality, interests, activities and social contacts. Only 11% were "really well adjusted and completely free from all kinds of mental disorders" at the time of follow-up. Good outcome was associated with good physical health, continuing work and living outside institutions. Life expectancy was significantly reduced in the depressed sample (5.1% reduction in men and 7.6% in women). This was accounted for almost completely by a suicide rate in depressives seven to eight times that in the general population.

Depressions starting in old age

Hospital studies

The studies by Christie (1982) and by Blessed & Wilson (1982) presented six-month and two-year follow-up figures on subjects admitted as in-patients to Crichton Royal Hospital between 1974 and 1976, and to St Nicholas' Hospital during 1976, respectively. Both studies found that approximately three-quarters of the subjects with affective psychoses were living in the community at six months and about two-thirds were in the community at two years. Only a small proportion had died within six months but about one-fifth were dead by two years. Discharge rate at both intervals was considerably higher than that reported by Roth (1955) from Graylingwell Hospital, but Blessed & Wilson (1982) emphasised that in their study one in five of the patients with an affective psychosis had either not been discharged or had been readmitted by two years. They concluded that affective illness in old age is associated with considerable persisting morbidity.

Post (1972) provided a much more detailed follow-up study of depressed in-patients admitted under his own consultant care between 1965 and 1967 as well as a comparison with his own previous study of patients admitted 16 years earlier. Post emphasised that the more recent series probably consisted of patients with more severe or resistant illnesses since a much higher proportion (60.9% v. 14.8%) had been given treatment for their depression and had failed to respond before admission. The main findings of the study were that although duration of initial in-patient stay had decreased, the overall outcome between the two series was largely unchanged. In the more recent study, in which the follow-up period was three years, about one-quarter of the patients had made a lasting recovery, one-third had had one or more relapses but were recovered at the time of follow-up and one-third had persisting symptoms of depression. One-third of these had been continuously ill for the three years of follow-up. The incidence of dementia at follow-up (6.5%) was no higher than could be expected in a non-depressed population of that age. The factors most clearly associated with a poor prognosis were age over 70 and duration of unrelieved depression for more than two years before admission.

Murphy (1983) reported a one-year follow-up study of 124 depressed patients referred over the course of a year to the psychogeriatric services at the London Hospital and Goodmayes Hospital, suffering from a first episode of depression in old age and meeting research criteria for primary depression. Thirty-five per cent were well, 19% had relapsed, 29% remained ill throughout, 3% had developed dementia and 14% were dead. Severity of illness, physical ill health, duration of illness before admission, and the occurrence of severe, non-illness-related life events during the follow-up year were significant predictors of poor outcome. Interestingly, only one in ten of those subjects with depressive delusions had a good outcome whereas 70% of those with psychotic depressions without delusions did well. Although direct comparison with Post's (1972) study cannot be made because the follow-up period is different, Murphy's (1983) sample appears if anything to have fared somewhat worse.

Baldwin & Jolley (1986) followed 100 patients aged 65 and over who had been admitted with severe, non-neurotic depressive states over 42 to 104 months. Seventy-nine per cent fitted Murphy's criterion of a 'new' case (i.e. no previous episode of depression since the age of 60), although 46% of the whole group had a history of depression, and 35% had been in-patients. An interim appraisal at one year was made to allow comparison with the findings of Murphy (1983). Fifty-eight per cent of the whole sample (65% of 'new' cases) were well, 15% had relapsed but had been well for a substantial part of the year, and 18% had continuing symptoms. Only 8% had died. At the end of the follow-up 60% had either remained well throughout or had further episodes followed by complete recovery. Only 7% suffered continuous depressive symptoms. Male sex and poor physical health, whether at presentation or developing subsequently, were associated with a poorer prognosis, a finding consistent with a number of previous studies, but there was no relationship between initial presentation with delusions and subsequent outcome.

The comparability of these samples has been the subject of further recent debate in the correspondence columns of the *British Journal of Psychiatry*. Baldwin & Jolley (1987) have contended that their findings both at one-year and four-year follow-up represent a better outcome, particularly in terms of mortality, than the subjects studied by Murphy (1987) (26% v. 37% dead at four years), although Murphy herself maintained that there was little difference in outcome between the two groups.

The influence of treatment on prognosis in the depression of old age has received surprisingly little attention. Post (1972) commented on the similar prognosis of elderly depressed subjects under his care who were admitted before and after the introduction of antidepressant drugs, but considered that many good-prognosis or treatment-responsive patients now never reach hospital, having been treated effectively in general practice. No prospective studies of prophylactic antidepressants or lithium treatment in the depressed elderly have been published, although Abou-Saleh & Coppen (1983) report retrospectively that lithium was both well tolerated and effective in preventing relapse in elderly subjects. Somewhat more evidence is available concerning the long-term effects of ECT. Baldwin & Jolley (1986) have suggested that their relatively favourable outcome figures may be due to high usage of ECT (48%; 65% of delusional depressives). This hypothesis is given some support by a study from Southampton (Godber *et al*, 1987) of 163 elderly patients treated with ECT. At three-year follow-up 67 (41%) were free of depression, with another 33 (20%) showing only mild symptoms. Of the remainder, 50 (31%) had died and 13 (8%) were chronic (nine were chronically depressed and four had developed a dementia).

Community studies

Few community-based studies of the natural history of depression in old age have been undertaken. Gianturco & Busse (1978) followed up a sample of "normal elderly volunteers" for a total of 20 years. Of those subjects depressed when first seen, 87% had had at least one other depressive episode, and by the end of the 20-year period nearly three-quarters had had at least one episode of depression. Surprisingly, episodes of depression were related to financial status in women and physical health in men, but age, sex and marital status did not seem related to likelihood of becoming depressed. MacDonald (personal communication) in a nine-month follow-up of patients attending their general practitioners found that of those depressed when first seen, one-third had improved and two-thirds remained depressed; during the nine-month follow-up 12% of those initially well had become depressed.

Copeland (personal communication) has recently completed a three-year follow-up study of 1070 subjects originally surveyed by Copeland *et al* (1987*a*). A preliminary analysis of the 89 subjects fulfilling AGECAT criteria for depressive neurosis showed that 9% refused to participate in the follow-up, 20% had died, 3% had developed a dementia, 26% were still depressed (6% worse, 17% unchanged and 3% improved), and 42% had recovered. Only 4% had been treated with antidepressants. Of the much smaller group of 32 subjects with depressive psychosis, the mortality was the same but the prognosis was somewhat poorer, with 31% still depressed and only 22%

recovered. This is in keeping with Murphy's (1983) finding that depressive delusions in old age were associated with poor outcome.

It is clear that there is considerable persistent morbidity associated with the depressions of old age. Prognosis has been reported to be related to symptom profile and to a variety of social variables and to physical health. Perhaps most importantly there is a strong suggestion that, in appropriate cases, an energetic approach to physical treatment and prophylaxis can beneficially affect outcome.

Conclusion

The depressions of old age are common, disabling, and present considerable problems in diagnosis and management. Only a small minority of elderly subjects with significantly dysphoric mood fulfil DSM-III criteria for MDE. Some of the remainder fulfil some or all of the criteria for dysthymic disorder. A considerable population with significant depressive symptoms fits poorly into DSM-III pigeonholes. The prognosis of severe depressions in old age is quite gloomy despite strong suggestions that aggressive treatment can reap dividends. The classification, management and prognosis of the much more frequent minor depressions of old age require considerable further study.

Symposium discussion

PROFESSOR HAMILTON: Dr Katona, you described certain features or symptoms characteristic of depression in the old aged, but it seems to me that some of them are more characteristic of old age than depression. The patients are somewhat querulous, a little disgruntled, they are hypochondriacal, they are resentful of others, but old people, as they get more and more handicapped and more and more unable to get around and do things, do begin to resent the fact that they are like that and others are not, I would have thought. Do you have any reasonable evidence that these features which you describe as depression in old age are really quite distinct from old age as such?

DR KATONA: It certainly seems to be true that these symptoms are commoner in elderly people than in younger people. On the other hand, I think the story is in a way analogous to that of dementia. Dementia becomes increasingly common with increasing age, but it remains manifestly the case that most old and very old people are not demented. I think there is a degree of disability from these depressive symptoms that is enough to say, "Well, this is not just old age, this is disabling enough not to be complacent about it". It is something where if one recognises it as a disabling or disease entity, one is more likely to be able to intervene appropriately. If one looks at it as purely a function of normal ageing, it is a sort of therapeutic nihilism.

So I would agree with you that yes, ageing brings with it more dissatisfaction and disgruntlement, but it does more than that. It brings a cluster of those things which for some, but by no means all elderly people, causes a very real disability. I think those people are ill in the lay sense.

DR TYRER (*chairman*): I should just like to comment that Max (Professor Hamilton) has got much less querulous and much calmer and shows none of those features as you have got older.

DR BERGMAN: I would like to support Dr Katona and deny what Professor Hamilton said because in our survey in Newcastle I looked at the normals as well and those people who had an absence of or very minimal affective symptoms had low scores for hypochondriasis, for complaints about loneliness, and for dissatisfaction, probably comparable with those of younger people. I do not think that people in helping professions who see only the dependent elderly are capable of making judgements about the normal elderly.

References

ABOU-SALEH, M. T. & COPPEN, A. (1983) The prognosis of depression in old age: the case for lithium therapy. *British Journal of Psychiatry*, **143**, 527–528.

AKISKAL, H. S. (1983) Dysthymic disorder: psychopathology of proposed chronic depressive subtypes. *American Journal of Psychiatry*, **140**, 11–20.

AMERICAN PSYCHIATRIC ASSOCIATION (1980) *Diagnostic and Statistical Manual of Mental Disorders* (3rd edn) (DSM–III). Washington, DC: APA.

ANGST, J. (1981) Clinical indicators for a prophylactic treatment of depression. *Advances in Biological Psychiatry*, **7**, 218–230.

BALDWIN, R. C. & JOLLEY, D. J. (1986) The prognosis of depression in old age. *British Journal of Psychiatry*, **149**, 575–583.

—— & —— (1987) Prognosis of depression in old age. *British Journal of Psychiatry*, **151**, 129.

BEDFORD, A., FOULDS, G. A. & SHEFFIELD, B. F. (1976) A new personal disturbance scale. *British Journal of Social and Clinical Psychology*, **15**, 387–394.

BEN-ARIE, O., SWARTE, L. & DICKMAN, B. J. (1987) Depression in the elderly living in the community: its presentation and features. *British Journal of Psychiatry*, **150**, 169–174.

BERGMANN, K. (1971) The neuroses of old age. In *Recent Developments in Psychogeriatrics: A Symposium* (eds D. W. K. Day & A. Walk). *British Journal of Psychiatry*, special publication no. 6.

BLAZER, D. & WILLIAMS, C. D. (1980) Epidemiology of dysphoria and depression in an elderly population. *American Journal of Psychiatry*, **137**, 439–444.

BLESSED, G. & WILSON, I. D. (1982) The contemporary natural history of depression in old age. *British Journal of Psychiatry*, **141**, 59–67.

BORSON, S., BARNES, R. A., KUKULL, W. A., *et al* (1986) Symptomatic depression in elderly medical outpatients. 1. Prevalence, demography, and health service utilization. *Journal of the American Geriatrics Society*, **34**, 341–347.

BULBENA, A. & BERRIOS, G. E. (1986) Pseudodementia: facts and figures. *British Journal of Psychiatry*, **148**, 87–94.

CHEAH, K-C., BALDRIDGE, J. A. & BEARD, O. W. (1979) Geriatric evaluation unit of a medical service: role of a geropsychiatrist. *Journal of Gerontology*, **34**, 41–45.

—— & BEARD, O. W. (1980) Psychiatric findings in the population of a geriatric evaluation unit: implications. *Journal of the American Geriatrics Society*, **28**, 153–156.

CHRISTIE, A. B. (1982) Changing patterns in mental illness in the elderly. *British Journal of Psychiatry*, **140**, 154–159.

CIOMPI, L. (1969) Follow-up studies on the evolution of former neurotic and depressive states in old age: clinical and psychodynamic aspects. *Journal of Geriatric Psychiatry*, **3**, 90–106.

COPELAND, J. R. M. (1981) What is a case, a case for what? In *What is a Case? The Problems of Definition in Psychiatric Community Surveys* (eds J. R. King, P. Bebbington & L. N. Robins), pp. 7–11. London: Grant McIntyre.

——, DEWEY, M. E. & GRIFFITHS-JONES, H. M. (1986) A computerized psychiatric diagnostic system and case nomenclature for elderly subjects: GMS and AGECAT. *Psychological Medicine*, **16**, 89–99.

——, ——, WOOD, N., *et al* (1987*a*) Range of mental illness among the elderly in the community: prevalence in Liverpool using the GMS-AGECAT package. *British Journal of Psychiatry*, **150**, 815–823.

——, GURLAND, B. J., DEWEY, M. E., *et al* (1987*b*) Is there more dementia, depression and neurosis in New York? A comparative community study of the elderly in New York and London using the community diagnosis AGECAT. *British Journal of Psychiatry*, **151**, 466–473.

DALLOSSO, H., MORGAN, K., EBRAHIM, S., *et al* (1986) Health and contact with medical services among the elderly in Greater Nottingham. *East Midland Geographer*, **9**, 37–44.

FOLSTEIN, M. F., FOLSTEIN, S. E. & MCHUGH, P. R. (1975) "Mini-mental state": a practical method for grading the cognitive state of patients for the clinician. *Journal of Psychiatric Research*, **12**, 189–198.

FREEDMAN, N., BUCCI, W. & ELKOWITZ, E. (1982) Depression in a family practice elderly population. *Journal of the American Geriatrics Society*, **30**, 372–377.

GIANTURCO, D. T. & BUSSE, E. W. (1978) Psychiatric problems encountered during a long-term study of normal ageing volunteers. In *Studies in Geriatric Psychiatry* (eds A. D. Issacs & F. Post), pp. 1–16. New York: John Wiley.

GILLIS, L. S. & ZABOW, A. (1982) Dysphoria in the elderly. *South African Medical Journal*, **62**, 410–413.

GODBER, C., ROSENVINGE, H., WILKINSON, D., *et al* (1987) Depression in old age: prognosis after ECT. *International Journal of Geriatric Psychiatry*, **2**, 19–24.

GOOD, W. R., VLACHONIKOLIS, I., GRIFFITHS, P., *et al* (1987) The structure of depressive symptoms in the elderly. *British Journal of Psychiatry*, **150**, 463–470.

GRIFFITHS, R. A., GOOD, W. R., WATSON, N. P., *et al* (1987) Depression, dementia and disability in the elderly. *British Journal of Psychiatry*, **150**, 482–493.

GURLAND, B. J. (1976) The comparative frequency of depression in various adult age groups. *Journal of Geronotology*, **31**, 283–292.

HALE, W. D. (1982) Correlates of depression in the elderly: sex differences and similarities. *Journal of Clinical Psychology*, **38**, 253–257.

HAMILTON, M. (1960) A rating scale for depression. *Journal of Neurology, Neurosurgery and Psychiatry*, **23**, 56–62.

HASEGAWA, K. (1985) The epidemiological study of depression in late life. *Journal of Affective Disorders* (suppl. 1), S3–S6.

JACOBY, R. J. & LEVY, R. (1980) Computed tomography in the elderly: 3. Affective disorder. *British Journal of Psychiatry*, **136**, 270–275.

KATONA, C. L. E. & ALDRIDGE, C. R. (1985) The dexamethasone suppression test and depressive signs in dementia. *Journal of Affective Disorders*, **8**, 83–89.

KAY, D. W. K., BEAMISH, P. & ROTH, M. (1964) Old age mental disorders in Newcastle upon Tyne. Part I: A study of prevalence. *British Journal of Psychiatry*, **110**, 146–158.

—— & BERGMANN, K. (1980) Epidemiology of mental disorders among the aged in the community. In *Handbook of Mental Health and Ageing* (eds J. E. Birren & R. B. Slone), pp. 34–56, Englewood Cliffs: Prentice-Hall.

——, HENDERSON, A. S., SCOTT, R., *et al* (1985) Dementia and depression among the elderly living in the Hobart community: the effect of diagnostic criteria on the prevalence rates. *Psychological Medicine*, **15**, 771–778.

KIVELA, S-L., NISSINEN, A., TUOMILEHTO, J., *et al* (1986) Prevalence of depressive and other symptoms in elderly Finnish men. *Acta Psychiatrica Scandinavica*, **73**, 93–100.

KRAL, V. A. (1983) The relationship between senile dementia (Alzheimer type) and depression. *Canadian Journal of Psychiatry*, **28**, 304–306.

LALIVE D'EPINAY, C. J. (1985) Depressed elderly women in Switzerland: an example of testing and generating theories. *Gerontologist*, **25**, 597–604.

LINN, M. W., HUNTER, K. & HARRIS, R. (1980) Symptoms of depression and recent life events in the community elderly. *Journal of Clinical Psychology*, **36**, 675–682.

MACDONALD, A. J. D. (1986) Do general practitioners "miss" depression in elderly patients? *British Medical Journal*, **292**, 1365–1367.

—— & DUNN, G. (1982) Death and the expressed wish to die in the elderly: an outcome study. *Age and Ageing*, **11**, 189–195.

MANN, A. H., GRAHAM, N. & ASHBY, D. (1984) Psychiatric illness in residential homes for the elderly: a survey in one London borough. *Age and Ageing*, **13**, 257–265.

MENDLEWICZ, J. (1976) The age factor in depression illness: some genetic considerations. *Journal of Gerontology*, **31**, 300–303.

MOORE, J. T. (1985) Dysthymia in the elderly. *Journal of Affective Disorders* (suppl. 1), S15–S21.

MORGAN, K., DALLOSSO, H. M., ARIE, T., *et al* (1987) Mental health and psychological well-being among the old and the very old living at home. *British Journal of Psychiatry*, **150**, 801–807.

MURPHY, E. (1982) Social origins of depression in old age. *British Journal of Psychiatry*, **141**, 135–142.

—— (1983) The prognosis of depression in old age. *British Journal of Psychiatry*, **142**, 111–119.

—— (1987) The prognosis of depression in old age. *British Journal of Psychiatry*, **150**, 268.

MURRELL, S. A., HIMMELFARB, S. & WRIGHT, K. (1983) Prevalence of depression and its correlates in older adults. *American Journal of Epidemiology*, **117**, 173–185.

MYERS, J. K., WEISSMAN, M. M., TISCHLER, G. L., *et al* (1984) Six-month prevalence of psychiatric disorders in three communities. *Archives of General Psychiatry*, **41**, 959–967.

NEUGARTEN, B. L., HAVIGHURST, R. J. & TOBIN, S. S. (1961) The measurement of life satisfaction. *Journal of Gerontology*, **16**, 134–143.

POST, F. (1972) The management and nature of depressive illness in late life: a follow-through study. *British Journal of Psychiatry*, **121**, 393–404.

—— & SHULMAN, K. (1985) New views on old age affective disorders. In *Recent Developments in Psychogeriatrics No. 1* (ed. T. Arie). London: Churchill Livingstone.

RAYMOND, E. F., MICHALS, T. J. & STEER, R. A. (1980) Prevalence and correlates of depression in elderly persons. *Psychological Reports*, **47**, 1055–1061.

REFLEFF, L. S. (1977) The CES–D scale: a self-rating depression scale for research in the general population. *Applied Psychological Measure*, **1**, 385.

ROTH, M. (1955) The natural history of mental disorder in old age. *Journal of Mental Science*, **101**, 281–301.

SALZMAN, C. (1985) Clinical guidelines for the use of antidepressant drugs in geriatric patients. *Journal of Clinical Psychiatry*, **46**, 38–44.

SNAITH, R. P., AHMED, S. N., MEHTA, S., *et al* (1971) Assessment of the severity of primary depressive illness: the Wakefield self-assessment depression inventory. *Psychological Medicine*, **1**, 143–149.

WANG, R., TRUBS, S. & ALBERNO, L. (1975) A brief self-assessing depression scale. *Journal of Clinical Pharmacology*, **15**, 163–167.

WEISS, I. K., NAGEL, C. L. & ARONSON, M. K. (1986) Applicability of depression scales to the old person. *Journal of the American Geriatrics Society*, **34**, 215–218.

WING, J. K., COOPER, J. E. & SARTORIUS, N. (1974) *The Measurement and Classification of Psychiatric Symptoms*. London: Cambridge University Press.

WORLD HEALTH ORGANIZATION (1978) *Mental Disorders: Glossary and Guide to their Classification in Accordance with the Ninth Revision of the International Classification of Diseases* (ICD–9). Geneva: WHO.

ZUNG, W. K. (1965) A self-rating depression scale. *Archives of General Psychiatry*, **12**, 63–66.

6 Personality and dysthymia

ROBERT M. A. HIRSCHFELD

In the mid-19th century, Karl Kahlbaum described depression in individuals with no history of mania which he deemed 'dysthymia' (Jackson, 1986). The extent to which these people suffered from chronic characterological problems is not clear. Chronic depression was of considerable interest to Kraepelin. He described a depressive temperament which he believed was the personality from which manic-depressive illness developed. This notion of a depressive spectrum was shared by other European clinical writers, such as Kretschmer, who considered dysthymia to predispose to manic-depressive illness.

In the United States the predominant historical approach to dysthymia has been psychodynamic, and chronic depression was described in terms of neurosis. The publication DSM-III (American Psychiatric Association, 1980) marked a major shift in American approaches to diagnosis. In DSM-III the term 'dysthymia' replaced 'depressive neurosis' to describe chronic milder depressions. This diagnostic category included patients who had long been described by clinicians as suffering from a depressive character, conveying a disorder of personality at least separate from, but more likely intertwined with, episodic psychopathology. The reason for the change was to describe the condition without the aetiological attributions connoted by the term 'neurosis'. The diagnostic category is a broad one, encompassing many subtypes which are unspecified in DSM-III. Several authors have proposed classification approaches to dysthymia, most notably Akiskal (1983).

Dysthymia is considered now to be an affective disorder, and not a personality disorder. Therefore the personality of these patients can be considered separately. This chapter provides an overview of the ways in which personality may relate to dysthymia, and presents some data on this issue. The data come from the Clinical Studies of the National Institute of Mental Health Collaborative Program on the Psychobiology of Depression (the collaborative programme), a longitudinal multicentre study of affective disorders.

Personality and dysthymia

The relationship between personality and dysthymia can be conceptualised in four ways (see Table 6.1). (a) Personality features may predispose to dysthymia. (b) The expression of certain personality features and dysthymia may lie on the same genetic spectrum. (c) Dysthymia may best be conceived of as a personality disorder, and its expression involves abnormal personality. (d) Personality features can be changed by the experience of living with dysthymia, being a complication of the disorder.

In the predisposition approach, personality features may precede the development of dysthymia, and be involved in its pathogenesis. In this situation personality presumably is an aetiological factor. This issue has been the subject of much thought and writing by clinical theorists, ranging from psychoanalytic to cognitive to behavioural. Psychoanalytic contributions have stressed undue interpersonal dependency (Chodoff, 1972; Hirschfeld *et al*, 1976), a quality in which one's self-esteem is excessively reliant on approval, attention, reassurance, and love from other people. Individuals with undue interpersonal dependency have insufficient internal and other resources to draw upon during times when attention from others wanes or terminates and, during these times, according to the theory, depression ensues. Cognitive theorists, such as Beck (1972), describe basic cognitive schema developed early in life that predispose to depression later in life.

The expression of certain personality features and dysthymia may lie on the same genetic spectrum. Here personality features and dysthymia may have no aetiological relationship, but are associated with one another because of their joint heritability due to some third factor. This possibility has received relatively little attention in the research literature because of methodological and other difficulties. Preliminary results from one study suggest that early-onset dysthymia may be genetically related to major depression (Klein *et al*, 1988). Another study of identical twins in Norway (Torgersen, 1984) did not find increased concordance for dysthymia, as has been found for bipolars.

Dysthymia may best be conceptualised as a disorder of character, that is, as a personality disorder. In this situation the personality features are part of the disorder itself and are indistinguishable from it. Indeed dysthymia has been deemed as 'depressive character' by many in the past.

The final type of relationship is the complication hypothesis, the opposite of the predisposition approach. In the complication hypothesis personality

TABLE 6.1
Relationship between personality and dysthymia

Predisposition	Personality features may predispose to dysthymia
Spectrum	Personality features and dysthymia may lie on the same genetic spectrum
Personality disorder	Dysthymia may be a personality disorder
Complication	Dysthymia may change personality

features do not predispose to the disorder, but rather are *themselves* changed by the dysthymia. This may make sense if one imagines what living for two or more years with lowered self-esteem, poor energy level, general pessimism, and insomnia. Surely this could easily change one's general outlook.

A difficulty in testing these last two approaches is interpretation of a positive change in personality that may be associated with successful treatment of the dysthymia. The positive personality change may reflect constructive growth resulting from the treatment techniques employed, particularly with psychotherapy. However, it is just as plausible that the therapy may have lifted the veil of the dysthymia to reveal the 'true' underlying character. This argument would more likely be made by psychopharmacologists. It would be very helpful in such a situation to have measures of personality obtained both *before* the onset of dysthymia and *after* full recovery from it due to treatment. Such a task would be very difficult, requiring ascertainment of a very large sample early in life, and following it for many years. Age effects on personality measures would have to be considered.

Evidence for the relationship between personality and dysthymic disorder from the collaborative programme

The collaborative programme is a joint research project between the NIMH and five major university hospitals in the United States (Columbia University in New York, Harvard University in Boston, Rush Medical School in Chicago, University of Iowa in Iowa City, and Washington University in St Louis). The purposes of the study are to evaluate approaches to the classification of affective disorders, to elucidate the clinical course of depression, to examine genetic and familial factors, and to investigate the role of psychosocial factors in the depression.

The collaborative programme is a naturalistic, prospective study of in-patients and out-patients with moderate to severe depression or mania presenting for treatment at one of the five participating medical centres. The study is *not* a clinical trial, in which patients are randomly assigned to specified treatment conditions. Rather, a patient's treatment is determined by his or her individual physician interacting with the patient and family.

All patients were evaluated with the Schedule for Affective Disorders and Schizophrenia (SADS; Spitzer & Endicott, 1979); Research Diagnostic Criteria (RDC; Spitzer *et al*, 1977); and other standardised instruments at index and have been followed for over five years.

Sample

Nine hundred and fifty-five in-patients and out-patients were admitted to the study. In addition, 2284 first-degree relatives of these patients were evaluated by interview and self-report independent of the proband. The current analyses involve personality data of relatives and patients who had fully recovered from their affective disorder at the time of their personality assessment with the exception of double-depressed patients, as described below. Assessments of patients occurred at a one-year follow-up examination. Relatives were assessed upon entry to the study.

The analyses involved three groups of relatives and two groups of patients. The first group included 63 relatives who had *recovered* from dysthymia and had *no* lifetime history of major depressive disorder. The second group included 25 *double-depressed* patients who had recovered from major depressive disorder but continued to suffer from dysthymia. Patients were considered to have double depression if they had a major depressive disorder superimposed on a pre-existing dysthymia of at least two years' duration (Keller & Shapiro, 1982). The third group comprised 139 patients who had recovered from major depressive disorder and had *no* history of dysthymia. The fourth group included 526 relatives who had *recovered* from a major depressive episode and had *no* history of dysthymia. The fifth group was 1275 relatives with no current or past psychiatric illness.

Assessments

Patients and relatives completed a personality battery composed of items from several different self-report inventories as part of their index evaluation. The same battery was completed again by patients at a one-year follow-up evaluation. Among these were the neuroticism and extraversion scales of the Maudsley Personality Inventory (MPI; Eysenck, 1962). The neuroticism scale measures general emotional stability, emotional responsiveness and a predisposition to neurotic breakdown under stress. Extraversion refers to outgoing, uninhibited, impulsive and sociable inclinations.

Sociodemographic data

Sociodemographic characteristics of the four diagnostic groups are presented in Table 6.2. Overall comparisons show significant differences on age, sex and marital status, while level of educational achievement does not differ between groups.

Differences in mean age between relatives who have never had a psychiatric illness (42.2 years) and relatives with a history of major depressive disorder (39.6 years) account for the finding of overall significance. While this difference is statistically significant, it is not clinically significant. The mean ages of all five groups are actually quite similar.

As expected, the ratio of men to women in the four clinical groups is approximately 1:2 with the exception of the probands recovered from major depressive disorder in which the ratio is 2:3. Within the sample of relatives who had never had a psychiatric illness, the sexes are almost equally represented, with a slight majority of women.

TABLE 6.2
Demographic characteristics of four diagnostic groups

	Dysthymic relatives (n = *63*)	*Double-depressed patients (recovered MDD)* (n = *25*)	*Recovered MDD patients* (n = *139*)	*Recovered MDD relatives* (n = *526*)	*Never ill relatives* (n = *1275*)
Age[1]*: years					
mean	41.5	40.2	39.6	39.6	42.2
s.d.	15.6	14.6	15.1	15.5	17.5
Sex[2]**					
male: %	32	32	40	31	46
female: %	68	68	60	69	54
Marital status**					
married or living together: %	65	56	52	65	70
unmarried: %	35	44	48	35	30
Education					
secondary or less: %	52	48	47	31	46
tertiary: %	48	52	53	69	54

MDD = Major depressive disorder.
1. Analysed using the *F*-statistic.
2. Analysed using the χ^2 statistic.
*Overall comparison of means significant at $P<0.02$.
**Overall comparison of means significant at $P<0.0001$.

Marital status also differs between groups with patients less likely to be married than relatives ($P<0.0001$), regardless of clinical status.

Statistical analyses

One-way analyses of variance (ANOVAs) with age and sex as covariates were used to compare the neuroticism and extraversion scores of the five diagnostic groups. Pairs of means within these analyses were compared using Tukey's Studentised range test since this test uses an experimentwise error term. The overall test of age differences was also done using a one-way ANOVA with Tukey's range test used in the further comparison of pairs of means. The χ^2 statistic was used to assess overall differences in sex, marital status and educational achievement between groups. Differences between pairs of groups were analysed using Fisher's exact test (two-tailed).

Results

The results are presented in Table 6.3. Relatives who had recovered from dysthymia and double-depressed patients still suffering from dysthymia scored significantly higher on the neuroticism scale than the other three groups. Non-double-depressed patients recovered from major depression scored near the published norms, while relatives with a history of major

TABLE 6.3
Maudsley Personality Inventory scores for five diagnostic groups

Scales	*Dysthymic relatives* (n = *63*) *(A)*	*Double-depressed probands (recovered MDD)* (n = *25*) *(B)*	*Recovered MDD probands* (n = *139*) *(C)*	*Recovered MDD relatives* (n = *526*) *(D)*	*Never-ill relatives* (n = *1275*) *(E)*
Neuroticism*					
mean	29.6	29.0	22.0	20.5	12.8
s.d.	11.0	12.2	12.5	12.1	10.3
Summary of Tukey's Studentised range test ($P<0.05$)			A,B>C,D>E		
Extraversion/introversion*					
mean	19.0	20.2	25.2	26.6	28.3
s.d.	10.7	10.3	9.5	10.0	9.1
Summary of Tukey's Studentised range test ($P<0.05$)		A,B,>C,D>E		B<D<E	

*Overall comparison of means significant at $P<0.0001$.

depression scored slightly below. The relatives with no history of psychiatric illness scored significantly below all the other groups, suggesting significantly greater emotional strength and resilience.

Similarly, on the extraversion scale the recovered dysthymic relatives and currently dysthymic patients were significantly more introverted than all other groups. The non-double-depressed patients recovered from a major depression were introverted compared with the national published norms, but were much less so than the dysthymics, as were the relatives who had recovered from major depression. The relatives who had never been ill had normal levels of extraversion.

These results indicate that individuals suffering from dysthymia have extremely abnormal personalities. They have extremely low levels of emotional strength and are likely to break down under stress. They are likely to be moody and fearful. They are very introverted and shy, avoiding social interactions. Their personalities are significantly more disturbed than those of individuals who have suffered only from major depression.

We do not have pre-morbid measures, and therefore cannot answer the predisposition versus complication questions. However, we can say something about the personality disorder issue. The relatives with dysthymia who had recovered from their affective disorders were almost indistinguishable from patients with double depression who had recovered from the major depression, but were still dysthymic when their personality was assessed. This strongly suggests that the abnormal personality features are independent from the dysthymia because they exist even after recovery.

Therefore, therapeutic approaches, both psychotherapeutic and pharmacological, should be attempted with these patients. Perhaps some of the cognitive or behavioural techniques which have been shown to be so successful among various patient groups might be helpful with these chronically disturbed patients.

Whether these personality features play a role in the pathogenesis or pathophysiology of dysthymia is unclear. It may well be that whatever is causing these personality abnormalities is also driving the dysthymia.

This group of patients has received relatively little attention in the research literature, especially compared with patients suffering from major depression. Kocsis & Frances (Kocsis *et al*, 1985; Kocsis & Francis, 1987) described a double-blind imipramine/placebo clinical trial in a group of 27 out-patients suffering from chronic depression, most of whom would meet criteria for dysthymia. Over half (7/13) of the imipramine-treated patients recovered, whereas only 2 of 14 placebo-treated patients recovered.

Conclusion

Patients suffering from dysthymia have very disturbed personalities, evidencing both increased neuroticism and introversion. These abnormalities persist even after recovery from the dysthymia.

Symposium discussion

DR CHECKLEY: Dr Hirschfeld, we are all very interested in those dysthymic relatives and the fact that they did not get depressed and did get better and they were different in that respect from ours. Did you have any independent evidence that they were like other dysthymic patients? The question in my mind is, are they actually dysthymic? Do you have any completely independent clinical measures that would suggest that they had anything else in common with other dysthymic populations, apart from meeting the operational criteria?

DR HIRSCHFELD: All of these dysthymic relatives of subjects were interviewed by experienced clinicians using the Schedule for Affective Disorders in Schizophrenia (SADS), so I am quite confident that they did indeed have dysthymia. The issues that you are addressing are intriguing and at the moment I do not have much more information on these people. I want to go carefully over their clinical state. I also do not have any information on whether they ever sought treatment: that is one thing that is different from the patients. Every single patient in our study had sought treatment and that is how we ascertained them, but the relatives might just have been living with this and I would like to look at the personality features of those who have had treatment and those who have not had treatment.

DR SCOTT: I wonder if Dr Hirschfeld could tell us whether he had had a chance to look at the personality variables by sex, because Weissman *et al* (1978) found that chronic depressives had a high neuroticism score, but that was true primarily of the female patients. I think it has been true in a number of other studies which looked at personality variables that neuroticism was particularly important in females but did not seem to be applicable to the male population.

In the Newcastle study, we found a similar trend, that the female patients scored higher on the EPI, on the neuroticism scale, but not the male patients (Scott, 1988).

DR HIRSCHFELD: That is an excellent point. Just the norms alone are different between men and women, and indeed in all the groups we looked at there were differences between men and women, pretty much in all of them.

In other papers I have written, I have separated them out. We decided this time to put them together and then statistically to adjust for sex, and for smaller differences with age. That makes the results easier to present and I think easier to interpret. There were no individual results that were true for only one sex and not the other: they were quite consistent, even though the levels were a little different.

PROFESSOR PAYKEL: You were careful to draw, at least by implication, a distinction between personality, which you were measuring, and mood state, but do you think that neuroticism as a personality measure is distinct from dysthymia? If you look at the detailed items in that scale, which I too have found to be a very useful scale in depression, a number of them are about mood lability. So I wonder if the personality that is characteristic of dysthymia *is* dysthymia. I do not think that can be true for introversion, but I wonder about neuroticism.

DR HIRSCHFELD: That is another excellent question. At one time we tried to develop a depression-free neuroticism scale and came up with zero items—every single one of them correlated highly with the depressive symptoms. That is not true of the extraversion scale and indeed these people are very isolated as well and it is also not true of the interpersonal dependency scale. If it were only neuroticism I would be more concerned, but even there, I am impressed with the findings because compared with the recovered major depressed patients, they have much higher neuroticism scores. So the disentangling of personality features, personality abnormalities as part of personality disorders, and mood state affective disorder diagnosis is very thorny. I am thinking about trying something else in my next research career!

DR CROW: Could I ask Dr Hirschfeld a question about the normal relatives in the catchment area study? I think I heard you describe them as showing increased resilience and I wondered if that was right. More generally, do you know how representative of the general population they are? Are there any particular characteristics with regard to social class or occupation which might distinguish these affective relatives from the normal population?

DR HIRSCHFELD: Are you asking about the affected relatives or unaffected relatives?

DR CROW: Unaffected.

DR HIRSCHFELD: Actually no, the unaffected relatives are not representative of the general population. In fact, their scores on the neuroticism scale are astoundingly different: they are much more healthy than the norms for the neuroticism scale on the Maudsley Personality Inventory, although their extraversion scales are right on the norm. So these people are especially strong and they have had no history of any psychopathology—they are a different group from a general population sample. That is quite clear. But we think they are an interesting group for contrast because we can say with assurance that they are not psychiatric patients. They span a wide social class—they would not be comparable to many of the Camberwell studies, but they are much more representative of the general social class.

DR TYRER (chairman): I wonder whether we have all been looking in the wrong place in trying to find dysthymia in patients—perhaps we should all be looking at the relatives.

References

AKISKAL, H. S. (1983) Dysthymic disorder: psychopathology of proposed chronic subtypes. *American Journal of Psychiatry*, **140**, 11–20.

AMERICAN PSYCHIATRIC ASSOCIATION (1980) *Diagnostic and Statistical Manual of Mental Disorders* (3rd edn) (DSM–III). Washington, DC: APA.

BECK, A. T. (1972) *Depression: Causes and Treatment*. Philadelphia: University of Pennsylvania Press.

CHODOFF, P. (1972) The depressive personality: a critical review. *International Journal of Psychiatry Medicine*, **27**, 196–217.

EYSENCK, H. J. (1962) *The Maudsley Personality Inventory*. San Diego: Educational and Industrial Testing Service.

HIRSCHFELD, R. M. A., KLERMAN, G. L., CHODOFF, P., *et al* (1976) Dependency—self-esteem—clinical depression. *Journal of the American Academy of Psychoanalysis*, **4**, 373–388.

JACKSON, S. W. (1986) *Melancholia and Depression*. New Haven: Yale University Press.

KELLER, M. B. & SHAPIRO, R. W. (1982) Double depression: superimposition of acute depressive episodes on chronic depressive disorders. *American Journal of Psychiatry*, **139**, 438–442.

KLEIN, D. N., TAYLOR, E. B., DICKSTEIN, S., *et al* (1988) The early–late onset distinction in DSM–III–R dysthymia. *Journal of Affective Disorders*, **14**, 25–33.

KOCSIS, J. H., FRANCES, A., MANN, J. J., *et al* (1985) Imipramine for treatment of chronic depression. *Psychopharmacology Bulletin*, **21**, 698–700.

— & — (1987) A critical discussion of DSM–III dysthymic disorder. *American Journal of Psychiatry*, **144**, 1534–1542.

SCOTT, J., BARKER, W. A. & ECCLESTON, D. (1988) The Newcastle chronic depression study: patient characteristics and factors associated with chronicity. *British Journal of Psychiatry*, **152**, 28–34.

SPITZER, R. L., ENDICOTT, J. E. & ROBINS, E. (1977) *Research Diagnostic Criteria for a Selected Group of Functional Disorders* (3rd edn). New York: Biometrics Research Division, New York State Psychiatric Institute.

— & — (1979) *Schedule for Affective Disorders and Schizophrenia (SADS)* (3rd edn). New York: Biometrics Research Division, New York State Psychiatric Institute.

TORGERSEN, S. (1984) Genetic and nosologic aspects of schizotypal and borderline personality disorders: a twin study. *Archives of General Psychiatry*, **41**, 546–554.

WEISSMAN, M. M., PRUSOFF, B. A. & KLERMAN, G. L. (1978) Personality and the prediction of long-term outcome of depression. *American Journal of Psychiatry*, **135**, 797–800.

7 Social adjustment in dysthymia

GIOVANNI B. CASSANO, GIULIO PERUGI, ICRO MAREMMANI and HAGOP S. AKISKAL

In recent years there has been remarkable progress in our understanding of the biological underpinnings of affective disorders. At the same time attempts have been made to delineate the psychosocial factors that influence vulnerability to depression. Loss of significant objects during childhood or adolescence (Birtchnell, 1970; Brown & Harris, 1978), life events with a significant individual impact (Paykel *et al*, 1969), and social support (Lin & Dean, 1984) have been identified as factors that can influence the development and the course of depressive disorder. Current evidence indicates that biological factors may predispose to psychosocial disruptions, which in turn could precipitate or maintain affective episodes (Akiskal, 1986). Furthermore, the availability of more efficacious and specific therapeutic modalities now allows treatment and monitoring of the majority of depressed out-patients in their family and work settings. This means that careful evaluation of the psychosocial setting of affective illness is assuming greater clinical significance.

Present trends in research on affective disorders are pragmatically orientated towards immediate usefulness in clinical practice, and remarkable findings concerning characteristic symptoms, course of illness, and response to treatment have resulted. On the other hand, studies of the adjustment of depressed patients in their various social roles and of their domestic and interpersonal dynamics are less numerous. Although DSM-III-R (American Psychiatric Association, 1987) considers the maximum degree of social adjustment attained in the year preceding a depressive episode an important prognostic sign, few objective attempts have been made to characterise social adjustment patterns. The existing sparce literature is largely limited to the interpersonal difficulties (Botwell & Weissman, 1977) and marital problems seen in depressed patients (Weissman & Paykel, 1974; Merikangas *et al*, 1985). In an earlier report we investigated a fuller spectrum of social functions in depressives with different degrees of recovery (Delisio *et al*, 1986). Our findings suggested that work and leisure functions were particularly disturbed. This chapter extends those findings with special reference to chronic depressions and their differentiation from anxiety states.

Social deficits in depressives with different degrees of recovery

Deficits during index evaluation

In order to assess the relationship between depressive illness and social adjustment, 176 patients with mild to moderate depressions were evaluated by the Social Adjustment Scale (SAS; Schooler *et al*, 1979). The sample characteristics were as follows: mean age ($\pm$ s.d.) = 53 $\pm$ (14), 79% female, 61% with major affective and 39% with dysthymic disorders by DSM–III criteria (American Psychiatric Association, 1980); 17% were new admissions to the ambulatory service and 83% were patients already enrolled in maintenance treatment.

The SAS items are scaled from 1 (good adjustment) to 4 (severe maladjustment), and the range of mean values (1.5–2.6) shown in Fig. 7.1 indicates mild to moderate impairment; work and leisure functions were, on average, the most disturbed areas.

We were interested in the types of social maladjustment at different levels of severity of symptoms of depression assessed on the Self-Assessment of Depression inventory (SAD), which has been standardised (Cassano & Castrogiovanni, 1977). As shown in Table 7.1, there was a significant linear relationship between symptom level measured on the SAD and social maladjustment in the five areas assessed by the SAS, except the degree of

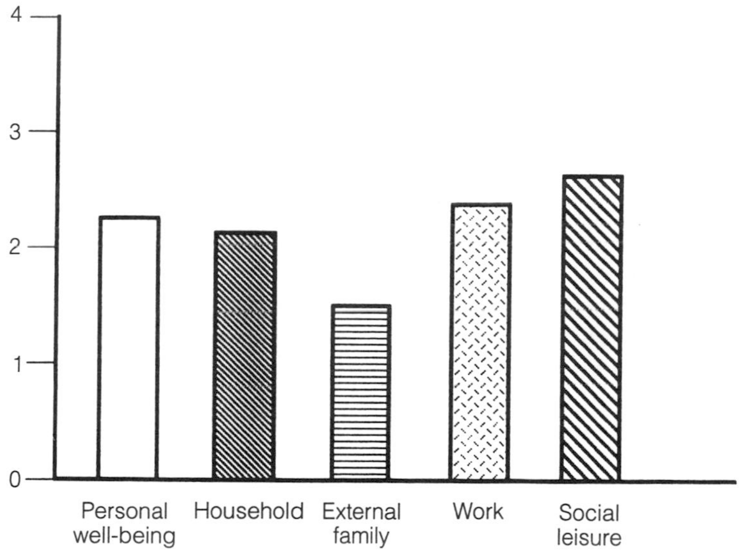

Fig. 7.1. SAS scores in social adjustment areas at index evaluation of 176 depressed out-patients

TABLE 7.1
Level of depression and social maladjustment at index evaluation

SAS areas	*Symptom level on SAD*					
	(A) *asymptomatic* (n = *35)*	*(B)* *mild* (n = *60)*	*(C)* *moderate* (n = *52)*	*(D)* *severe* (n = *29)*	R[1]	F
Work (1)	1.8	2.3	2.7	2.8	0.50	19.35
Household (2)	1.7	2.0	2.3	2.4	0.42	12.11
Relationships outside family (3)	1.2	1.4	1.6	1.7	0.30	7.57
Social/leisure (4)	2.4	2.5	2.7	3.0	0.28	6.04
Personal well-being (5)	1.8	2.1	2.4	2.7	0.53	23.29

1. Correlations between SAS areas and SAD total score analysed by Pearson's *R*.
The Schefee's multiple range test shows differences ($P<0.05$) as follows: (1) A v. B v. C = D, (2) A v. B = C v. D, (3) A v. C = D, (4) A = B v. D, (5) A v. B. v. C = D.

linearity was less pronounced in the areas of social/leisure activities and relationships with the people outside the family. It is also noteworthy that those patients who had recovered to a relatively asymptomatic level showed relatively little evidence of social maladjustment except in the area of social/leisure activities; in this respect they were at least as impaired as those with mild-to-moderate symptomatic depression.

An especially interesting finding was that the work and social/leisure areas seemed differentially affected by the severity of depression. Thus, patients with relatively few depressive symptoms manifested much difficulty in their leisure activities, but relatively little at work; patients with more depressive symptoms showed significant maladjustment in both work and leisure.

Deficits during follow-up

As these data were collected cross-sectionally and not longitudinally, verification of the findings from a longitudinal perspective seemed essential. Thus, we assessed the social adjustment of 99 (56%) of the patients in the original sample in a longitudinal three-month follow-up. During this interval all patients received a tricyclic antidepressant (amitriptyline, nortriptyline or imipramine) plus a benzodiazepine in modest doses, as necessary. Supportive psychotherapeutic attention was given to patients' immediate familial and vocational problems.

Changes in social adjustment by patients whose symptoms improved were compared with those who did not improve during the three-month interval. Patients whose depression improved also showed a general tendency to improve more in social adjustment (Table 7.2). Overall statistically significant change in the improvers, however, was found only in the work and personal well-being areas of the SAS. Remission of depressive episodes appeared to be accompanied by better social adjustment in work skills and relationships, and in feelings of personal well-being. Since the personal well-being area of the SAS contains items exploring depressive features, it is not surprising that improvement in depressive symptoms is accompanied by improvement in this area.

TABLE 7.2
Adjusted means at three months and improvement in depression

SAS area	*Improvers* (n = *56*)	*Non-improvers* (n = *43*)	F
Work	2.3	2.5	4.86**
Personal well-being	2.0	2.2	7.57***
Household relationships			
principal household member	1.8	2.0	NS
sexual adjustment	3.2	3.5	NS
parental role	1.6	1.7	NS
household concerns	1.8	1.9	NS
Relationships outside family	1.4	1.5	NS
Social/leisure			
leisure activities	3.6	3.6	NS
social contacts	2.3	2.6	3.29*
interpersonal contacts	1.9	2.0	NS

*$P<0.10$, **$P<0.05$, ***$P<0.01$.

Relationships with the principal household member and adjustment to the parental role, however, appeared less influenced by the waning of the depressive episode. Most importantly, greater remission of depressive symptoms was not accompanied by significantly greater improvement in social/leisure activities. Adjustment during leisure-time pursuits remained markedly impaired even after significant improvement in depressive pathology.

Patients whose depression remained stationary or worsened according to the SAD measure did not change significantly in any of the social adjustment areas during the three-month interval. Thus, mean scores in the different social adjustment areas were essentially unchanged after three months, confirming a pattern of continued maladjustment. Maladjustment was most marked in the areas of leisure activities, sexual adjustment, and work.

These data support the notion that classic depression masked by somatic symptoms is increasingly replaced by depressive syndromes masked by uneasiness at work, by disagreements with coworkers, and by difficulties in maintaining stable relationships. By contrast, the capacity to use and enjoy leisure time appeared less related to variation in depressive symptoms (Cassano *et al*, 1983). While it is not possible to be definite, our findings suggest that impairment of the capacity to enjoy leisure may represent a trait marker present during the depressive patient's lifetime. Alternatively, impaired ability to enjoy leisure may be a residual feature of depressive episodes.

Patients appear to pass through different states of social readjustment as they improve. The most refractory area is that of regaining the ability to enjoy leisure-time activities.

Deficits in acute versus chronic depression

In a comparison of patients diagnosed with dysthymic disorders with episodic depressions (Table 7.3), the SAS revealed greater social maladjustment in

TABLE 7.3
SAS means for episodic depression and dysthymic disorders

	Episodic (n = *92)*	*Dysthymic* (n = *68)*	P
SAS areas			
work	2.3	2.5	0.05
household relationships	2.0	2.2	0.03
relationships outside family	1.5	1.5	NS
social/leisure	2.6	2.6	NS
personal well-being	2.3	2.2	NS
SAS factors			
personal anguish	2.0	2.2	0.03
intimate relations	3.2	2.9	NS
parental role	1.9	2.0	NS
primary relationship	1.7	2.4	0.03
work affect	2.4	2.6	NS
sexual practices	2.7	2.7	NS
major role performances	2.3	2.5	NS
self-care	1.5	1.5	NS
economic independence	2.3	2.3	NS
social relationship	2.4	2.6	NS

TABLE 7.4
SAS means for unipolar episodes, dysthymic disorder and depression with panic disorder

SAS areas	*Unipolar* (n = *39)*	*Dysthymic* (n = *29)*	*Panic* (n = *37)*	F
Work	2.5	2.4	1.9	4.46*
Personal well-being	2.4	2.2	2.0	3.02*
Household relationships				
principal household member	1.8	1.9	1.8	NS
sexual adjustment	2.6	2.8	1.8	5.25**
parental role	1.9	1.5	1.4	NS
household concerns	2.0	2.1	1.7	NS
Relationships outside family	1.5	1.6	1.5	NS
Social/leisure				
leisure activities	3.5	4.0	2.9	5.68**
social contacts	2.3	2.7	2.3	NS
interpersonal contacts	1.9	2.3	1.6	7.31**

*$P<0.05$, **$P<0.01$. The Schefee's multiple range test shows significant differences as follows: panic v. unipolar = dysthymic.

the former. Thus, dysthymics had greater disturbance in the work and household areas. Maladjustment in the domains of work and family suggest that the pre-existing role structure is of little help in social re-adjustment when the depressive disorder has assumed a chronic course. Equally, elevated scores in the social/leisure area in the chronic and episodic depression further suggests that chronicity does not contribute additional impairment in this area, thereby further supporting the trait nature of this disturbance.

Deficits in depressive versus anxious patients

The data in Table 7.4 suggest that the social adjustment deficits are specific for primary depressive illness. Thus, depressions secondary to panic disorder showed relatively little evidence for social maladjustment in work, leisure activities, and interpersonal contact; as expected, sexual adjustment and personal well-being, areas sensitive to depression, were also minimally affected. Overall, primary depressives appear impaired in social areas that require effort, motivation and anticipation of pleasure, functions relatively intact in subjects with anxiety disorders.

Discussion

While it is customary to emphasise interpersonal difficulties in the clinical evaluation of depressed patients, our data showed impairment not only in intimate and sexual relations, but also in work and leisure activities—indeed, the latter two functions appeared more disturbed than the other areas of adjustment.

Our data suggest that work and leisure activities exhibit different time patterns with respect to the course of the depressive episode. It would appear that at the onset of depression one of the significant signs of illness is alteration in the degree of liking for and interest in one's job. Although impairment in leisure activity was apparent at the onset of depression, it tended to persist even after the depressive episode had subsided to an asymptomatic level. Continued impairment of leisure activities during remission suggests that depression is a chronic illness and that social dysfunction persists into this phase in subtle but measurable form. In line with previous theoretical formulations (Akiskal & McKinney, 1973, 1975; Klein, 1974), we would hypothesise that impairment of capacity to enjoy leisure activities represents a trait disturbance in depressive illness reflecting altered central hedonic features.

As expected, social disturbances were more pronounced in all areas in chronic depressives, including areas with predetermined social structures (work and family).

Study of the social adjustment of patients during depression and in other psychopathological conditions can be of great interest for the psychiatrist. Better knowledge of the specific areas of social adjustment that are most compromised by episodes of different mental disorder can be useful for diagnosis, therapy, and rehabilitation. Such an approach allows one to see the patient in daily life, to identify more clearly the problems produced by the illness, and to select treatment interventions aimed at resolution of the difficulties.

Our findings indicate that maladjustment at work improves with antidepressant treatment, even if the depressive episode is not completely resolved. Incapacity to manage leisure time, however, appears to remain at least well past the peak period of depression. This suggests that feelings of inadequacy in work may signal that depression is becoming acute. Such complaints alert psychiatrists to make an early diagnosis and timely therapeutic interventions to allow the patient to make a normal adjustment to work. Also, therapist awareness of the difficulties depressed patients have enjoying leisure time even after the acute depression remits should orientate them towards therapeutic programmes that foresee the use of psychotherapy and social assistance. It would appear relevant to mention in this context the observations of Weissman *et al* (1979) to the effect that while pharmacological treatment is efficacious in the acute phase of depression and in the prevention of relapse, it may prove less effective for long-term full recovery in some areas of social adjustment compared with interpersonal psychotherapy.

We therefore submit, in conclusion, that better knowledge of specific areas of greatest social maladjustment should lead to better choices between types of rehabilitative interventions and methods of psychotherapy (cognitive, interpersonal, familial, behavioural, etc.).

Symposium discussion

DR TYRER (*chairman*): Thank you very much, Professor Cassano, for showing us that social adjustment can add very useful information to that available from clinical observation. You can have quite a lot of social impairment, whether or not you have any symptoms at all, as you have demonstrated.

DR MURPHY: I have a question for Professor Cassano. I was wondering if you could tell us as clinical psychiatrists what we could look for to see social maladjustments within our patients.

PROFESSOR CASSANO: If I understood your question correctly, the rating scale that we are using is the SAS rating scale. This scale allows us to explore different areas of social adjustment which are referred to the patient and the family members.

DR MURPHY: The reason why I asked the question is that the data that we have from our own study is such that I would like to say first of all that it was not a decent rating scale that we used, it was more a clinical impression gained from interviews with relatives and scoring "yes" or "no" on a variety of factors like marital adjustment, terminations of pregnancy, use of leisure time, social withdrawal, employment, conviction rates etc., number of jobs. We could find no difference whatsoever between the dysthymics and the major affectives, which was rather surprising. We were expecting there to be a nosologically easily clinically identifiable group and a distinctly handicapped group, but in fact that did not come out. May be it was the scales we were using to measure it.

DR TYRER (*chairman*): We have had an extremely interesting session which has demonstrated that dysthymic disorder is a far more complex issue than just collecting symptoms and ordering them in space and producing diagnostic categories. We have seen that it is difficult to define its chronological limits, we have seen that it has some very important personality aspects which are very difficult to separate from mental state. I think one of the troubles is, dysthymia being a long-term diagnosis and personality being a persistent characteristic, one of the main criteria we use to separate personality from mental state is its persistence. If we have a condition, a mental disorder which is persistent, it makes it extremely difficult.

We have also heard from Professor Cassano of the importance of social adjustment. This is really illustrating the boundary of the disorder, I would have preferred perhaps to entitle this the dysthymic syndrome, which is very similar to disorder, but at least it does not confine you so much to the mental state diagnosis.

References

AKISKAL, H. S. (1986) A developmental perspective on recurrent mood disorders: a review of studies in man. *Psychopharmacology Bulletin*, **22**, 579–586.

—— & MCKINNEY, W. T. (1973) Depressive disorders: toward a unified hypothesis. *Science*, **182**, 20–28.

—— & —— (1975) Overview of recent research in depression: integration of ten conceptual models into a comprehensive clinical frame. *Archives of General Psychiatry*, **32**, 285–302.

AMERICAN PSYCHIATRIC ASSOCIATION (1980) *Diagnostic and Statistical Manual of Mental Disorders* (3rd edn) (DSM-III). Washington, DC: APA

—— (1987) *Diagnostic and Statistical Manual of Mental Disorders* (3rd edn, revised) (DSM-III-R). Washington, DC: APA.

BIRTCHNELL, J. (1970) Early parent death and mental illness. *British Journal of Psychiatry*, **116**, 281–288.

BOTWELL, S. & WEISSMAN, M. M. (1977) Social impairment four years after an acute depressive episode. *American Journal of Orthopsychiatry*, **47**, 231–237.

BROWN, G. W. & HARRIS, T. (1978) *Social Origins of Depression*. London: Tavistock.

CASSANO, G. B. & CASTROGIOVANNI, P. (1977) *S.A.D., Scala di Autovalutazione per la Depressione*. In *La Condizione Depressiva* (ed. G. B. Cassano). Milan: Masson Italia Editore.

——, MAGINI, C. & AKISKAL, H. S. (1983) Short-term, subchronic, and chronic sequelae of affective disorders. *Psychiatric Clinics of North America*, **6**, 55–68.

DELISIO, G., MAREMMANI, I., PERUGI, G., *et al* (1986) Impairment of work and leisure in depressed outpatients. *Journal of Affective Disorders*, **10**, 79–84.

KLEIN, D. F. (1974) Endogenomorphic depression. *Archives of General Psychiatry*, **31**, 447–454.

LIN, N. & DEAN, A. (1984) Social support and depression. A panel study. *Social Psychiatry*, **19**, 83–91.

MERIKANGAS, K. R., PRUSOFF, B. A., KUPFER, D. J., *et al* (1985) Marital adjustment in major depression. *Journal of Affective Disorders*, **9**, 5–11.

PAYKEL, E. S., MYERS, J. K., DIENELT, M. N., *et al* (1969) Life events and depression: a controlled study. *Archives of General Psychiatry*, **21**, 753–760.

SCHOOLER, N. R., HOGARTY, G. E. & WEISSMAN, M. M. (1979) Social Adjustment Scale II. In *Resource Material for Community Mental Health Program Evaluators*, publication n [ADM 79-328] (eds W. A. Argreaves *et al*), pp. 290–330. Washington, DC: US Dept of Health, Education and Welfare.

WEISSMAN, M. M. & PAYKEL, E. S. (1974) *The Depressed Woman—A Study of Social Relations*. Chicago: University of Chicago Press.

——, PRUSOFF, B. A., DI MASCIO, A., *et al* (1979) The efficacy of drugs and psychotherapy in the treatment of acute depressive episodes. *American Journal of Psychiatry*, **136**, 55.

8 5HT and dysthymic disorder

J. F. W. DEAKIN

Dysthymia is a recent diagnostic concept and, as other contributors have pointed out, the diagnostic criteria identify a small group of patients. It is therefore not surprising that studies of the role of 5HT in dysthymia are almost non-existent.

Clinical studies presented in this book suggest that dysthymic patients are not a homogeneous group. Some appear to have subclinical major depressive illness, others go on to develop various anxiety states and in one subgroup there is evidence of non-affective personality difficulties and disorders. It therefore seems likely that any disturbances of 5HT function in depression and anxiety will be relevant to the genesis of dysthymic states.

5HT receptors

Recent years have seen major advances in receptor mechanisms involved in 5HT neurotransmission and these are summarised by Bradley *et al* (1986). Three main groups of 5HT receptors have been proposed (1,2 and 3), and $5HT_1$ receptors have been classified into 1a, b and c subtypes. Some $5HT_1$ receptors are located on 5HT neurons and exert an inhibitory influence on 5HT release. They can be regarded as sensors which monitor the extra-cellular concentration of 5HT and correct deviations by varying the degree of inhibition of release. Some $5HT_1$ receptors are post-synaptic and mediate some of the post-synaptic effects of 5HT which probably include formation of cyclic adenosine monophosphate (cAMP).

$5HT_2$ receptors are exclusively post-synaptic and do not modify 5HT release. Strangely, $5HT_2$ receptors do not become supersensitive (do not proliferate) after chronic treatment with antagonists. On the contrary, a prolonged subsensitivity (reduced number of receptor binding sites) is seen (Leysen *et al*, 1986). The mechanism of this unusual effect is unknown. Furthermore, there is evidence that destruction of 5HT neurons in rats does not induce a proliferation of $5HT_2$ receptors (Leysen *et al*, 1983; Quik &

Azmitea, 1983) although a study with small numbers of mice suggests that supersensitivity may occur in this species when 5HT is depleted by more than 70% (Heal *et al*, 1985).

$5HT_3$ receptors may be present in brain, and selective $5HT_3$ antagonists have recently been developed (e.g. Britain *et al*, 1987). As yet little is known about this 5HT receptor.

Neurobiological relationship between anxiety and depression

Symptoms of anxiety and depression commonly coexist and it is doubtful whether there is a categorical distinction between the two. A small proportion of patients may have pure symptoms of anxiety or depression but many have both. In patients presenting to their general practitioners Goldberg and Bridges (Chapter 9) have shown that their symptoms can be resolved into two dimensions which measure anxiety and depression. However, the two dimensions are highly correlated—the anxiety dimension is quite a good measure of severity of depression and the depression dimension is a good measure of the severity of anxiety. Anxiety and depression are separate but correlated dimensions of behavioural disturbance. One explanation of this is that the neurobiological bases of anxiety and depression are distinct but related processes.

In a classic formulation, Akiskal & McKinney (1975) showed how sociological, behavioural and analytical theories of depression had in common the central idea that depression involves a lost efficacy of rewards. This concept is enshrined in DSM–III where depressed mood includes a "pervasive loss of interests and pleasure" (American Psychiatric Association, 1980). Animal behavioural studies suggest that brain catecholamine neurons are concerned with the detection of reinforcers and in mediating their effects on learning and motivation (Deakin & Crow, 1986). Several lines of evidence suggest that deficient noradrenergic function occurs in depression (Schildkraut, 1965; Glass *et al*, 1984). Thus a deficiency of catecholamine neurotransmission may underlie the depressive's insensitivity to rewards (Stein, 1962).

Behavioural formulations suggest that anxiety involves a susceptibility to form conditioned fear responses (e.g. Gray, 1971). According to this view anxious subjects are excessively sensitive to aversive stimuli which exert an inappropriate degree of control over behaviour. There is a good deal of evidence that 5HT neurons are involved in mediating the effects of punishment on animal behaviour. This is largely based on the ability of experimental impairment of 5HT function to release behaviour from inhibition by aversive stimuli (Wise *et al*, 1970; Geller & Blum, 1970; Tye *et al*, 1977). It is not yet clear which 5HT receptor subtypes are involved in punishment processes, but $5HT_2$ receptor antagonists have antipunishment activity in some behavioural models (Colpaert *et al*, 1985; Critchley & Handley, 1986) and the $5HT_2$ receptor antagonist ritanserin shows anxiolytic activity in patients (Ceulemans *et al*, 1985). Recently developed $5HT_3$ receptor antagonists also show anxiolytic activity in animal models (Costall *et al*, 1987). Thus excessive 5HT neurotransmission, perhaps through $5HT_2$ receptors, may underlie the anxiety dimension in psychopathy.

The reason that anxiety and depression are separate dimensions of behavioural disturbance may thus lie in their distinct psychological and neurochemical bases. The reason the dimensions are correlated may be that reward and punishment, catecholamine and 5HT neurotransmission are reciprocally related processes.

Anxiety and depression: differential treatment response?

The close relationship between anxiety and depression would suggest that they respond to similar treatments. Two large trials in out-patients with admixtures of anxiety and depressive symptoms make this point (Johnstone *et al*, 1980; Kahn *et al*, 1986; see also Ancill *et al*, 1984). Both studies compared a benzodiazepine, a tricyclic antidepressant, or both, with placebo. As expected both found that symptoms of anxiety and depression were highly correlated. In both studies the tricyclic was more effective than the benzodiazepine in treating all categories of patient irrespective of whether anxiety or depression was the predominant symptom. The fact that imipramine is effective in the treatment of panic disorder (Klein, 1964) also highlights the lack of distinction between anxiety and depression in terms of response to treatment. The efficacy of benzodiazepines in treating anxiety is called into question by these and other trials. They probably do have minor short-term anxiolytic effects but there is evidence they have weak antidepressant actions too (Rickels *et al*, 1985).

The mechanism of the anxiolytic action of antidepressants is unknown. All established antidepressants cause a gradual decrease in number of $5HT_2$ receptors (Peroutka & Snyder, 1980) and it is tempting to speculate that this common property is related more directly to anxiolysis than to antidepressant efficacy in view of 5HT punishment theories. It is intriguing that the presence of anxiety is regarded as a contraindication to electroconvulsive therapy (ECT) (e.g. Carney *et al*, 1965) because, in contrast to antidepressants, ECT increases $5HT_2$ receptor numbers (Vetulani *et al*, 1981).

The role of 5HT in depression

Studies of 5HT neurotransmission in depression have yielded contradictory and inconsistent results (Table 8.1). Several studies have reported reduced concentrations of 5HIAA in cerebrospinal fluid (CSF) and post-mortem brain in depressed patients and suicide victims and this is the main evidence for 5HT deficiency theories of depression (Bourne *et al*, 1968; Sjostrom & Roos,

TABLE 8.1
Conflicting views on 5HT and depression

5HT excess	*5HT deficiency*
Increase in $5HT_2$ receptors in post-mortem brain	Low 5HIAA in cerebrospinal fluid Low imipramine binding
Acute antidepressants	
$5HT_2$ antagonism	5HT reuptake blockers
Amitriptyline	Citalopram
Mianserin	Fluoxetine
Trazodone	Fluvoxamine
Chronic antidepressants	
Decrease in $5HT_2$ receptor binding	Increase in 5HT effects on neuronal firing (?$5HT_1$)

1972; Goodwin *et al*, 1973; Asberg *et al*, 1976). However, there are negative results (e.g. Cooper *et al*, 1986; Gjerris *et al*, 1987). Stanley & Mann (1983) found increased $5HT_2$ receptor numbers in suicide post-mortem brain suggesting excessive rather than deficient 5HT neurotransmission in depression. However, these results have not been corroborated (Cooper *et al*, 1986; Ferrier *et al*, 1986).

It can be seen from Table 8.1 that evidence for 5HT deficiency theories applies to pre-synaptic 5HT neuron function whereas evidence for 5HT excess theories applies to post-synaptic $5HT_2$ receptors. In attempting to reconcile the conflicting evidence, it has been suggested that reduced release of 5HT causes the increase in $5HT_2$ receptor binding sites observed in some studies as a compensatory supersensitivity response (Meltzer *et al*, 1984). However, this is not an adequate explanation because $5HT_2$ receptors do not show supersensitivity when the 5HT input is reduced or destroyed (see above). It is possible that supersensitivity occurs when the loss of 5HT input is extreme (Heal *et al*, 1985) but such depletions are far in excess of the reductions in 5HIAA seen in some CSF studies. Another suggestion is that hypersensitive $5HT_2$ receptors cause feedback inhibition of 5HT release and thus the reduced CSF 5HIAA concentrations seen in some studies (Nagayama *et al*, 1981). Again this is not an adequate explanation because $5HT_2$ receptors do not influence 5HT release or synthesis.

To attempt to discriminate between conflicting 5HT excess and deficiency theories, Dr Ian Pennell and I have been using pituitary hormonal responses to intravenous loads of tryptophan as an *in-vivo* index of functional 5HT neurotransmission in depressed patients and controls. The method was described by Charney *et al* (1982).

5HT neuroendocrinology in depression

Subjects were administered 100 mg/kg of *l*-tryptophan intravenously after an overnight fast and an hour of bed rest. Blood samples were drawn

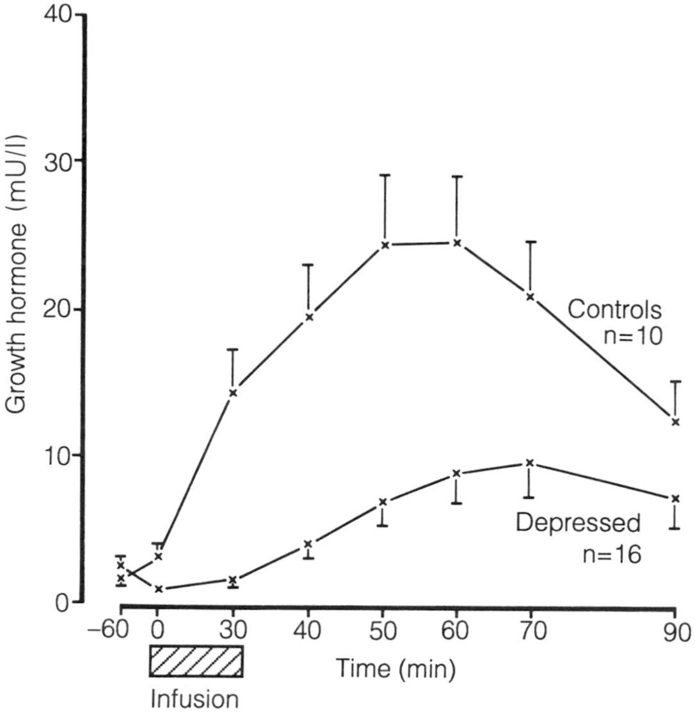

Fig. 8.1. Growth hormone responses to l*-tryptophan in control subjects* (n = *12) and patients* (n = *16) meeting DSM–III criteria for major depressive disorder. All patients were free of drugs for one month. Means* ± *s.e.m.*

at intervals before and after tryptophan loads and assayed for growth hormone (GH) and prolactin (PRL). No consistent cortisol response was seen.

Figures 8.1 and 8.2 show GH and PRL responses to tryptophan in 16 depressed patients (DSM–III major depressive disorder) and 12 controls. GH responses were very significantly attenuated in the depressed patients whereas the PRL response is not significantly reduced. However, weight loss has been shown to enhance PRL responses to tryptophan (Goodwin *et al*, 1987*a*) and when three patients with significant self-rated weight loss are removed from the analysis the reduction in PRL responses is significant.

Two other groups have reported reduced PRL responses to tryptophan in depression (Heninger *et al*, 1984; Cowen & Charig, 1987) and Siever *et al* (1984) found the same using fenfluramine, a drug which releases 5HT.

Differences in hormonal responses between depressed patients and controls are not attributable to differences in sex, age or menstrual status of females.

These results suggest that 5HT neurotransmission is reduced in depressed patients and appear to refute 5HT-excess theories. However, this interpretation assumes that hormonal responses to tryptophan are mediated by 5HT mechanisms.

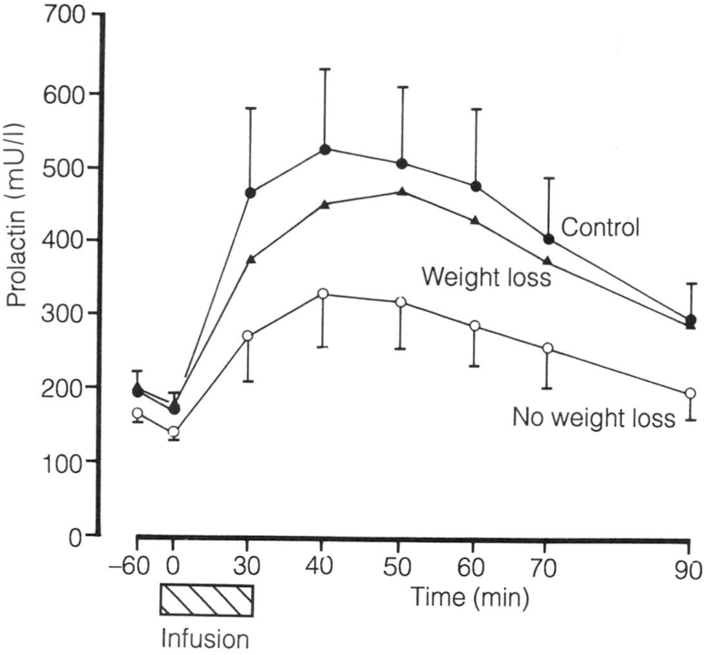

Fig. 8.2. Prolactin responses to l*-tryptophan in depressives with weight loss of more than 3 kg* (n = *3*) (▲——▲) *and with less than 3 kg weight loss* (n = *13*) (○——○), *and controls* (n = *12*) (●——●). *Means* ± *s.e.m.*

TABLE 8.2
Effect of ritanserin or placebo treatment on hormone responses to l*-tryptophan in two subjects*

	Peak hormone responses (mU/l)			
	Growth hormone		*Prolactin*	
	subject 1	*subject 2*	*subject 1*	*subject 2*
Placebo	10	36	53	218
Ritanserin	10	27	124	390

GH and PRL responses to tryptophan probably do involve 5HT receptors since normal subjects pre-treated with the 5HT reuptake inhibitor clomipramine show enhanced responses (Anderson & Cowen, 1986). We attempted to determine which receptor subtypes are involved by pre-treating normal subjects with 5HT antagonists. Figure 8.3 shows that the non-selective $5HT_1$ and $5HT_2$ receptor antagonist metergoline did not block the GH response. In two subjects the selective $5HT_2$ receptor antagonist ritanserin did not block the GH response (Table 8.2). Therefore $5HT_1$ and $5HT_2$ receptors do not appear to be involved in mediating GH responses to trytophan.

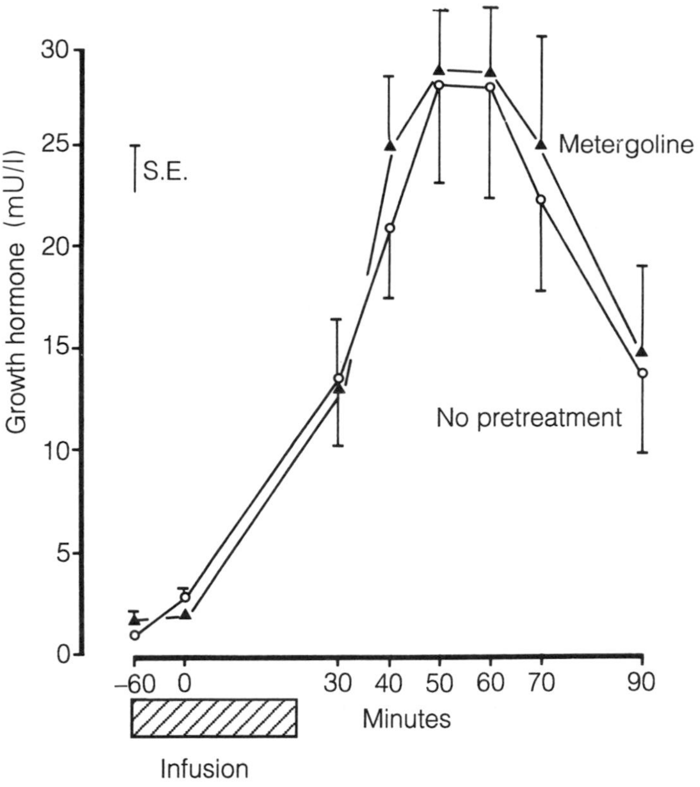

Fig. 8.3. Growth hormone responses of $5HT_1$ and $5HT_2$ to l*-tryptophan in four subjects tested twice, on one occasion with metergoline (▲——▲) and on the other with no pre-treatment (○——○). Means ± s.e.m.*

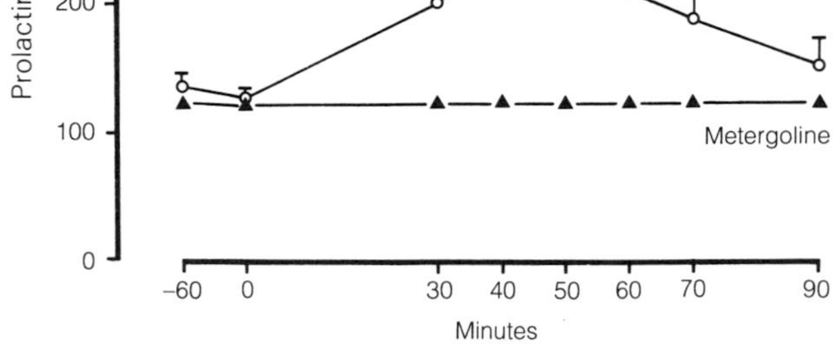

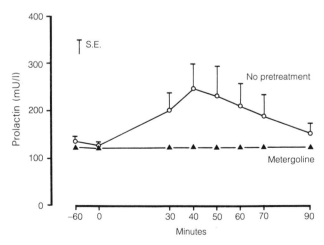

Fig. 8.4. Prolactin responses to l*-tryptophan in four subjects tested twice, on one occasion pre-treated with metergoline (▲——▲) and on the other with no pre-treatment (○——○). Means ± s.e.m.*

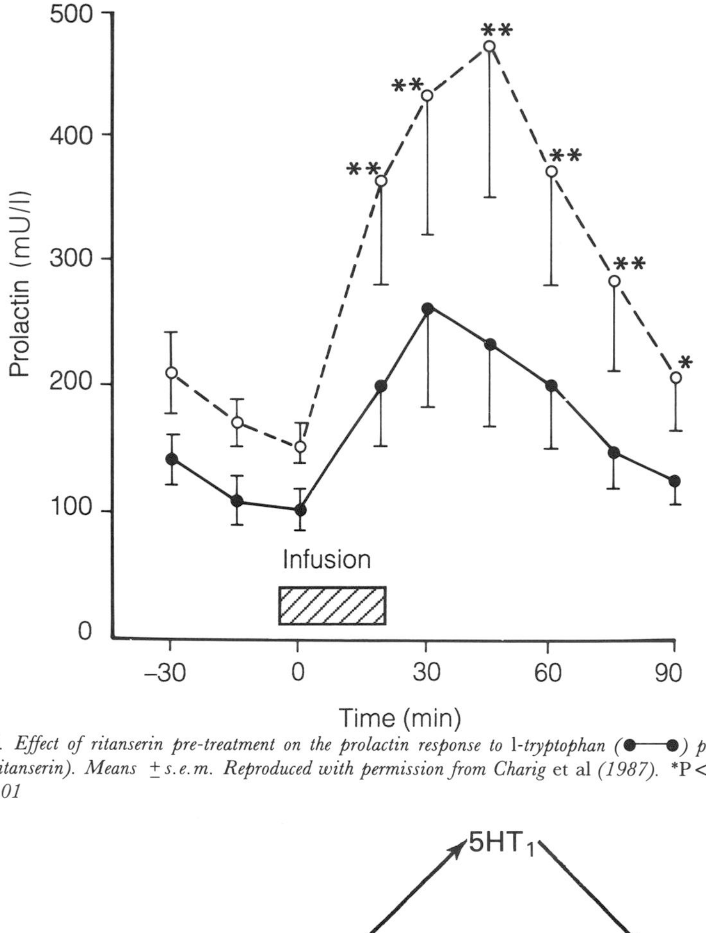

Fig. 8.5. Effect of ritanserin pre-treatment on the prolactin response to l*-tryptophan (●——●) placebo, ○---○ ritanserin). Means ± s.e.m. Reproduced with permission from Charig* et al *(1987).* *P < *0.05,* **P < *0.01*

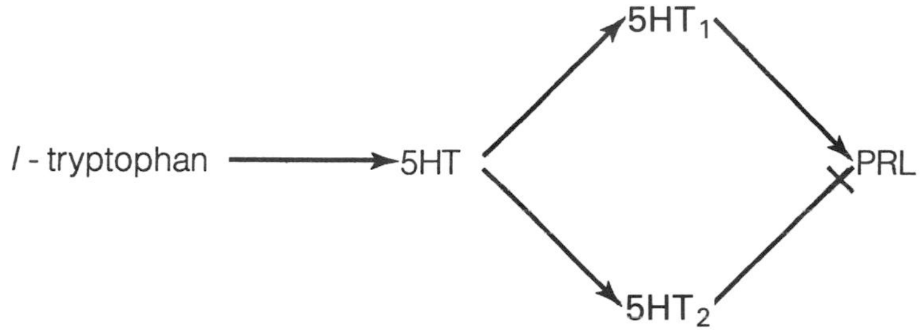

Fig. 8.6. 5HT receptor subtypes involved in PRL responses to l*-tryptophan. Ritanserin blocks* $5HT_2$ *receptors, removing an inhibitory component of 5HT upon PRL secretion thus potentiating PRL responses to* l*-tryptophan*

In four subjects metergoline abolished the PRL response (Fig. 8.4) and this result has been confirmed by Cowen *et al* (1987). In contrast, ritanserin, far from blocking PRL responses, caused a doubling in our two subjects (Table 8.2) and in the study of Charig *et al* (1987) (Fig. 8.5). These results indicate that PRL responses to tryptophan are mediated by $5HT_1$ receptors and suggest that $5HT_2$ receptors normally inhibit the response (Fig. 8.6).

TABLE 8.3

Reports of $5HT_2$ antagonists enhancing the effects of $5HT_1$

Effect on:	*Study*
Prolactin secretion	Charig *et al* (1987)
Neuronal firing	Lakoski & Aghajanian (1985)
RU24696 locomotion	Goodwin & Green (1985)
VIP[1] inhibition of cAMP	Weiss *et al* (1986)

1. Vasoactive intestinal polypeptide.

TABLE 8.5

Opposed effects of $5HT_1$ and $5HT_2$ receptors

Effect on:	*Study*
Sleep	Clarenbach *et al* (1987)
Sexual behaviour	Wilson & Hunter (1985)
Temperature regulation	Gudelsky *et al* (1986)
5HT syndrome	Harrison-Read (1983)
Morphine analgesia	Gonzalez & Stolz (1985)
Suprahyoid muscle twitching	Gardner *et al* (1987)

5HT receptor subtypes and depression

There are other reports that $5HT_2$ antagonists enhance responses mediated by $5HT_1$ receptors (Table 8.3) and several experimental situations where $5HT_1$ and $5HT_2$ receptors appear to exert opposed effects (Table 8.4). The mechanism proposed in Fig. 8.5 may therefore have a general applicability. This mechanism suggests that blunted PRL responses to tryptophan may come about in two ways: a deficiency in systems involving $5HT_1$ receptors or by an excessive inhibitory influence of $5HT_2$ receptors (Fig. 8.7). This reasoning raises the possibility that depression also involves an imbalance between reduced function in $5HT_1$ receptor systems and enhanced function in systems which have $5HT_2$ receptors.

This speculation may go some way towards reconciling 5HT-deficiency and 5HT-excess theories of depression. As noted in Table 8.1, evidence for 5HT-excess theories applies to $5HT_2$ receptors—increased $5HT_2$ receptors in suicide post-mortem brain and the ability of antidepressants to block or down-regulate $5HT_2$ receptors. If, as some CSF studies suggest, 5HT release is reduced in depression this would reduce the tone of $5HT_1$ receptors more than that of $5HT_2$ receptors if the latter are abnormally numerous in depression.

It is striking that many antidepressants have actions which would tend to reverse the proposed imbalance in 5HT receptor function. All effective

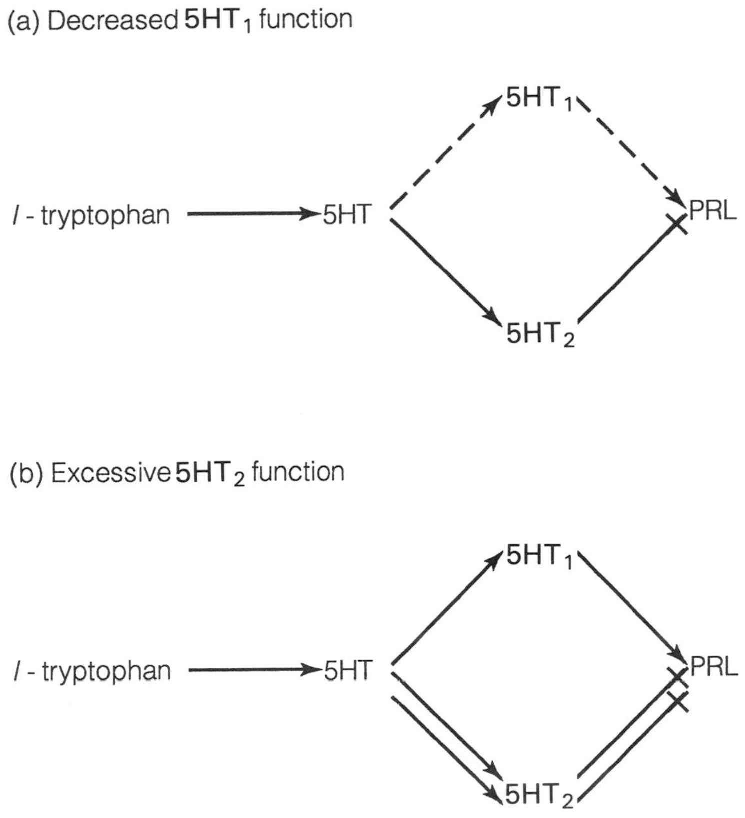

Fig. 8.7. Two mechanisms for blunted PRL responses to l-*tryptophan in depression*

antidepressants are either $5HT_2$ receptor antagonists or induce $5HT_2$ receptor down-regulation. Electrophysiological experiments suggest that chronic antidepressant therapy may enchance $5HT_1$-receptor-mediated effects. Iontophorectically applied 5HT inhibits the firing of forebrain units. In animals which have been chronically treated with an antidepressant, forebrain units become more sensitive to 5HT (De Montigny & Aghajanian, 1984). This may indicate an enhanced functioning of $5HT_1$-like receptors since the $5HT_1$ agonist 8OHDPAT mimics the effects of 5HT in this system (Mason, 1985). The fact that the $5HT_2$ antagonist ketanserin enhances electrophysiological effects of 5HT suggests the $5HT_2$ receptors restrain the $5HT_1$-like effects (Lakoski & Aghajanian, 1985). Thus the reduction in $5HT_2$ receptors caused by antidepressant treatment may be the explanation of the enhanced electrophysiological effects of 5HT in antidepressant-treated animals. In summary, the ability of long-term antidepressants to enhance 5HT effects on neuronal firing suggests either a potentiation of $5HT_1$ receptor function or a $5HT_2$ antagonist-like action. However, caution is needed in linking 5HT receptor binding sites with electrophysiological actions of 5HT; at present there is not a neat correspondence between the two (De Montigny *et al*, 1984). For example, Goodwin *et al* (1987) report that the behavioural syndrome evoked by 8OHDPAT is markedly attenuated in rats chronically treated with antidepressants. Clearly, further studies are needed to elucidate the effects of antidepressants on the functioning of 5HT receptor subtypes.

In the light of the receptor imbalance idea, the pharmacology of atypical antidepressants is intriguing. Trazodone lacks effects on monoamine reuptake but is a $5HT_2$ receptor antagonist and has a metabolite (MCPP) which is a $5HT_1$ receptor agonist (Al-Yassiri *et al*, 1981; Fuller *et al*, 1981). Buspirone is an anxiolytic which may have significant antidepressant activity (Geller & Hartman, 1982). On repeated administration buspirone and other $5HT_1$ agonists induce $5HT_2$ receptor down-regulation (Blackshear *et al*, 1986; DeSouza *et al*, 1986). The $5HT_2$ receptor antagonist ritanserin appears to have anxiolytic activity (Ceulemans *et al*, 1985; Colpaert *et al*, 1985; Critchley & Handley, 1986).

It seems probable that selective 5HT reuptake blockers such as fluvoxamine have antidepressant activity (Amin *et al*, 1984) without differential effects upon 5HT receptor subtypes and this may be a problem for the 5HT receptor imbalance idea. However, there is evidence that these drugs may be less generally effective than conventional antidepressants (Norton *et al*, 1984; Danish University Antidepressant Group, 1986) and most have delayed actions on noradrenergic neurotransmission which may be relevant to their antidepressant activity (Claassen, 1983; Racagni & Bradford, 1984, unpublished conference presentation).

The psychobiology of affective disturbance reconsidered

The study of the behavioural functions of 5HT receptor subtypes has hardly begun and any theory is necessarily tentative. Hitherto, 5HT neurotransmission has been considered as a unitary mechanism in behavioural studies. Furthermore, classification of 5HT receptor subtypes remains preliminary and whether they are physiologically functional is disputed.

Psychological studies of the effects of aversive stimuli have primarily been concerned with motivation and learning. However, aversive stimuli also set in train adaptive responses which serve to minimise and protect against analgesia (stress-induced analgesia) and there is evidence that descending 5HT projections to the spinal cord are involved (Tricklebank *et al*, 1984). Perhaps ascending 5HT systems have a role in mediating resilience to repeated aversive stimuli and when such protective mechanisms break down the state of learned helplessness or depression develops.

Kennett *et al* (1985) have shown that when rats are subjected to two hours of immobilisation they are less active and defecate more when tested in an open field apparatus 24 hours later. However, after repeated daily immobilisation rats become tolerant to the stress and show no abnormalities in open-field behaviour. Such chronically stressed animals show enhanced behavioural stereotypes in response to drugs that act at $5HT_1$ receptors. These authors showed that the effects of acute stress on open-field behaviour could be prevented by treating rats with 8OHDPAT and other drugs that act as agonists at $5HT_1$ receptors and by antidepressants (Kennett *et al*, 1987). The results are compatible with the view that $5HT_1$ receptors are involved in adaptation to stress. It is interesting that in this model female rats show less tolerance to repeated stress and fail to develop enhanced behavioural responses to $5HT_1$ receptor agonists. Perhaps this is a model for the greater susceptibility of women to depression.

Depression, or in animals learned helplessness or behavioural despair, can be regarded as a failure of adaptive/protective responses to stress: in this mode, a failure of $5HT_1$ neurotransmission. There is evidence that learned helplessness is associated with reduced 5HT release and that experimentally increasing 5HT neurotransmission reverses it (Petty & Sherman, 1983; Sherman & Petty, 1980, 1982). There is some contrary evidence (Brown *et al*, 1982; Edwards *et al*, 1986; Soubrie *et al*, 1986) but none of the studies has used agents with selective actions on 5HT receptor subtypes.

The role of 5HT receptor subtypes in the genesis of anxiety is not clear. As discussed earlier, $5HT_2$ receptor antagonists appear to have anxiolytic activity but so do $5HT_3$ receptor antagonists. However, almost nothing is known of the distribution of $5HT_3$ receptors or of their function in the brain and so speculation of their role in anxiety is premature. It may be that $5HT_2$ or $5HT_3$ receptors mediate the conventionally studied effects of punishment on behaviour—animal behavioural models of anxiety or fear.

It is suggested the 5HT-punishment theories remain viable and relevant to clinical anxiety and depression but that there is a need for elaboration of these theories to take account of 5HT receptor subtypes and to include consideration of adaptive responses to punishment as well as its short-term effects. $5HT_2$ and $5HT_3$ receptors may mediate immediate fear and anxiety responses to aversive stimuli and post-synaptic $5HT_1$ receptors may be more concerned with the development of resilience to stress. Clinical anxiety may involve increased $5HT_2$ or $5HT_3$ receptor neurotransmission, and depression, which tends to be a later response to stress, may involve deficient function in $5HT_1$ receptor systems. This tentative reformulation is compatible with many of the biological findings in depression and with the pharmacology of antidepressant drugs—drugs that are effective in the treatment of anxiety as well as depression.

These ideas seem highly relevant to dysthymia, a subclinical depressive syndrome often accompanied by symptoms of anxiety. Whether distinct genetic, psychosocial and neurobiological mechanisms are involved in the genesis of lifelong dysthymic states as opposed to episodic illnesses remains to be elucidated.

Symposium discussion

DR CROW: Presumably you envisage these $5HT_1$ and $5HT_2$ receptors as both post-synaptic.

DR DEAKIN: Yes.

DR CROW: What happens at the cellular level? What are they doing in terms of cyclic nucleotides?

DR DEAKIN: Nobody knows what the secondary effects of $5HT_1$ and $5HT_2$ receptor stimulation are. $5HT_1$ receptors seem to induce cAMP formation. What $5HT_2$ receptors do is completely unknown. There is a recent suggestion that there may be an endogenous peptide which binds to that site, but it is not actually to do with 5HT synaptic neurotransmission at all but is a sort of indirect modulator of $5HT_1$ neurotransmission.

PROFESSOR CASSANO: Is the effect on $5HT_2$ long lasting or short lasting? Is there tolerance to this effect?

DR DEAKIN: Which effect do you mean?

PROFESSOR CASSANO: In blocking $5HT_2$ receptors; the antagonistic effect on $5HT_2$.

DR DEAKIN: Are you referring to the ability of $5HT_2$ antagonists to down-regulate $5HT_2$ receptors?

PROFESSOR CASSANO: Yes, by ritanserin.

DR DEAKIN: It is very strange that giving a 5HT antagonist actually causes a decrease in the number of $5HT_2$ receptors. You would expect a compensatory supersensitivity, which seems to happen with most other neuronal systems, but that does not happen with the $5HT_2$ receptor, which is one reason for thinking that it may not be a typical synaptic receptor. If you block the $5HT_2$ receptor, you get a decrease. A single dose of a $5HT_2$ antagonist will cause quite a long-lasting decrease in $5HT_2$ receptor binding. The mechanism of that is not completely understood.

DR KATONA: If you are postulating a single effect of $5HT_2$ antagonists, would that not predict that the therapeutic benefit would be instant in the way that one does not get with conventional antidepressants and which therefore throws cold water on the old explanations for re-uptake blockade and so on? Is that, in fact, clinically the case with ritanserin or related drugs?

DR DEAKIN: The trial of ritanserin that I was thinking of in anxiety states showed the usual gradual emergence of an anti-anxiety effect. I do not have a simple explanation for why acute blockade does not reverse what I propose as the psychological function of overactivity in that receptor. It may be that you just have to learn, and weaken your conditioned associations. You require further trials of experience with a new neurochemical setting at a lower level. You require experience with a lower level of 5HT neurotransmission in order to learn not to be anxious.

DR KATONA: Presumably an alternative explanation at receptor level would be that you cannot look at 5HT receptors in isolation. Perhaps you are seeing, let us say, the down-regulation of beta receptors that is a common property of most antidepressants.

DR DEAKIN: Sure. I just could not talk about catecholamines as well. I would see those acting primarily on the reinforcement hedonic side of the equation rather than on the anxiety side. The point is that it comes to the same thing in the end. Anxiety and depression are separate, but they are correlated, reciprocally related dimensions of disturbance.

PROFESSOR AKISKAL: The model you have presented is a very interesting one, but I would like to know how you would fit lithium into the picture, because it also has an effect on the serotonin system and has no anti-anxiety effects at all clinically.

DR DEAKIN: So little is known about what lithium does to 5HT neurotransmission. In electrophysiological studies it potentiates some of those neuronal effects of 5HT. It has effects on $5HT_1$ and $5HT_2$ receptors in some studies. It is a very confused picture. I cannot possibly fit it in. I am not sure I would agree that lithium does not do anything to anxiety.

PROFESSOR AKISKAL: How about ECT?

DR DEAKIN: That is interesting. People always throw that at me because, unlike antidepressant drugs, ECT increases $5HT_2$ neurotransmission, and so they say that down-regulation of $5HT_2$ receptors cannot be anything to do with the antidepressant effect because ECT ups it and antidepressants down it. You have to remember that they are very different patients that respond to ECT. In the Northwick Park trial it was only the psychotic depressives who showed the benefit of real ECT over simulated ECT, and there may be very different processes at work. I think that down-regulation of $5HT_2$ receptors, on the basis of the model, is more related to anti-anxiety effect. It is interesting that high levels of anxiety are a contra-indication to ECT. ECT makes it worse. Maybe it is because it increases $5HT_2$ neurotransmission.

References

AKISKAL, H. S. & MCKINNEY, Jr, W. T. (1975) Overview of recent research in depression: integration of ten conceptual models into a comprehensive clinical frame. *Archives of General Psychiatry*, **32**, 285–303

AL-YASSIRI, M. M., ANKIER, S. I. & BRIDGES, P. K. (1981) Trazodone—a new antidepressant. *Life Science*, **28**, 2449–2458.

AMERICAN PSYCHIATRIC ASSOCIATION (1980) *Diagnostic and Statistical Manual of Mental Disorders* (3rd edn) (DSM-III). Washington, DC: APA.

AMIN, M. M., ANANTH, J. V., COLEMAN, B. S., *et al* (1984) Fluvoxamine: antidepressant effects confirmed in a placebo-controlled international study. *Clinical Neuropharmacology*, **7**, 580–581.

ANCILL, R. J., POYSER, J., DAVE, A., *et al* (1984) Management of mixed affective symptoms in primary care: a critical experiment. *Acta Psychiatrica Scandinavica*, **70**, 463–469.

ANDERSON, I. M. & COWEN, P. J. (1986) Clomipramine enhances prolactin and growth hormone responses in *l*-tryptophan. *Psychopharmacology*, **89**, 131–133.

ASBERG, M., THONEN, P., TRASKMAN, L., *et al* (1976) 'Serotonin depression': a biochemical subgroup within the affective disorders. *Science*, **191**, 478–480.

BLACKSHEAR, M. A., MARTIN, L. L. & SANDERS-BUSH, E. (1986) Adaptive changes in the $5HT_2$ binding site after chronic administration of agonists and antagonists. *Neuropharmacology*, **25**, 1267–1271.

BOURNE, H. R., BUNNEY, W. E., COLBURN, R. W., *et al* (1968) Noradrenaline, 5-hydroxytryptamine and 5-hydroxyindoleacetic acid in hindbrains of suicidal patients. *Lancet*, *ii*, 805–808.

BRADLEY, P. B., ENGEL, G., FENUIK, W., *et al* (1986) Proposals for the classification and nomenclature of functional receptors for 5-hydroxytryptamine. *Neuropharmacology*, **25**, 563–576.

BRITTAIN, R. T., BUTLER, A., COATES, I. H., *et al* (1987) GR380327, a novel selective $5HT_3$ receptor antagonist. *British Journal of Pharmacology*, **90**, 87.

BROWN, L., ROSELLINI, R. A., SAMUELS, O. B., *et al* (1982) Evidence for a serotonergic mechanism of the learned helplessness phenomenon. *Pharmacology, Biochemistry and Behaviour*, **17**, 877–883.

CARNEY, M. W. P., ROTH, M. & CARSIDE, R. F. (1965) The diagnosis of depressive syndromes and the prediction of ECT response. *British Journal of Psychiatry*, **111**, 659–674.

CEULEMANS, D. L. S., HOPPENBROWERS, M. L. J. A., GELDERS, Y. G., *et al* (1985) The influence of ritanserin, a serotonin antagonist, in anxiety disorders: a double blind placebo-controlled study versus lorazepam. *Pharmacopsychiatry*, **18**, 303–305.

CHARIG, E. M., ANDERSON, I. M., ROBINSON, J. M., *et al* (1987) L-tryptophan and prolactin release: evidence for interaction between $5HT_1$ and $5HT_2$ receptors. *Human Psychopharmacology*, **1**, 93–97.

CHARNEY, D. S., HENINGER, G. R., RENHARD, J. F., *et al* (1982) Effect of intravenous L-tryptophan on prolactin and growth hormone and mood in healthy subjects. *Psychopharmacology*, **77**, 217–222.

CLAASSEN, V. (1983) Review of the animal pharmacology and pharmacokinetics of fluvoxamine. *British Journal of Clinical Pharmacology*, **15**, 349S–355S.

COLPAERT, F. C., MEERT, T. F., NIEMEGEERS, C. J. E., *et al* (1985) Behavioural and 5HT antagonist effects of ritanserin: a pure and selective antagonist of LSD discrimination in rat. *Psychopharmacology*, **86**, 45–54.

COOPER, S. J., OWEN, F., CHAMBERS, D. R., *et al* (1986) Post-mortem neurochemical findings in suicide and depression: a study of the serotonergic system and imipramine binding in suicide victims. In *The Biology of Depression* (ed. J. F. W. Deakin). London: Gaskell.

COSTALL, B., DOMANEY, A. M., KELLY, M. E., *et al* (1987) Anxiogenesis follows abstinence withdrawal from long-term treatment with diazepam but not GR28032F. *British Journal of Pharmacology*, **90**, 420p.

COWEN, P. J. & CHARIG, E. M. (1987) Neuroendocrine responses to tryptophan in major depression. *Archives of General Psychiatry*, **44**, 958–966.

CRITCHLEY, M. A. E. & HANDLEY, S. L. (1986) 5-HT_2 receptor antagonists show anxiolytic-like activity in the x-maze. *British Journal of Pharmacology*, **89**, 646P.

DANISH UNIVERSITY ANTIDEPRESSANT GROUP (1986) Citalopram: clinical effect profile in comparison with clomipramine. A controlled multicenter study. *Psychopharmacology*, **90**, 131–138.

DE MONTIGNY, C., BLIER, P. & CHAPAT, Y. (1984) Electrophysiological-identified serotonin receptors in the CNS. *Neuropharmacology*, **23**, 1511–1520.

DE MONTIGNY, C. & AGHAJANIAN, G. K. (1984) Tricyclic antidepressants: long-term treatment increases responsivity of rat forebrain neurones to serotonin. *Science*, **202**, 1303–1306.

DESOUZA, R. J., GOODWIN, G. M., GREEN, A. R., *et al* (1986) Effect of chronic treatment with $5HT_1$ agonist (8-OH-DPAT and RU24969) and antagonist (isapirone) drugs on the behavioural responses of mice to $5HT_1$ and $5HT_2$ agonists. *British Journal of Pharmacology*, **89**, 377–384.

DEAKIN, J. F. W. & CROW, T. J. (1986) Monoamines, rewards and punishment: the anatomy and physiology of the affective disorders. In *The Biology of Depression* (ed. J. F. W. Deakin), pp. 1–25. London: Gaskell.

EDWARDS, E., JOHNSON, J., ANDERSON, D., *et al* (1986) Neurochemical and behavioural consequences of mild, uncontrollable shock-effects of PCPA. *Pharmacology, Biochemistry and Behaviour*, **25**, 415–421.

FERRIER, I. N., MCKEITH, I. G., CROSS, A. J., *et al* (1986) Post mortem neurochemical studies in depression. *Annals of the New York Academy of Science*, **487**, 128–142.

FULLER, R. W., SNODDY, H. D., MASON, N. R., *et al* (1981) Disposition and pharmacological effects of m-chlorphenylpiperazine in rats. *Neuropharmacology*, **20**, 151–162.

GARDNER, C. R., GUY, A. P. & JAMES, V. (1987) Opposite effects of $5HT_1$ and $5HT_2$ agonists on suprahyoid muscle twitching. *British Journal of Pharmacology*, **91**, 471p.

GELLER, I. & HARTMAN, R. J. (1982) Effects of buspirone on operant behaviour of laboratory rats and cynomologus monkeys. *Journal of Clinical Psychiatry*, **40**, 25–29.

GELLER, N. E. & BLUM, K. (1970) The effects of 5-HTP on parachlorophenylalanine (P-CPA) attenuation of conflict behaviour. *European Journal of Pharmacology*, **9**, 319–324.

GJERRIS, A., SORENSON, A. S., RAFAELSEN, O. J., *et al* (1987) 5HT and 5HT1AA in cerebrospinal fluid in depression. *Journal of Affective Disorders*, **12**, 13–22.

GLASS, I. B., THOMPSON, C., CORN, T., *et al* (1984) The GH response to clonidine in endogenous as compared to reactive depression. *Psychological Medicine*, **14**, 773–777.

GONZALEZ, J. P. & STOLZ, J. F. (1985) Functional antagonism between subtypes of 5-hydroxytryptamine receptors on morphine antinociception. *British Journal of Pharmacology*, **85**, 248.

GOODWIN, F. K., POST, R. M., DUNNER, D. L., *et al* (1973) Cerebrospinal fluid amine metabolites in affective illness: the probenecid technique. *American Journal of Psychiatry*, **130**, 73–79.

GOODWIN, G. M., DESOUZA, R. J. & GREEN, A. R. (1987*b*) Attenuation by electroconvulsive shock and antidepressant drugs of 5HT1A receptor mediated hypothermia and serotonin syndrome produced by 8-OH-DPAT in the rat. *Psychopharmacology*, **91**, 500–505.

GOODWIN, G. M. & GREEN, A. R. (1985) A behavioural and biochemical study in mice and rats of putative selective agonists and antagonists for $5HT_1$ and $5HT_2$ receptors. *British Journal of Pharmacology*, **84**, 743–753.

GOODWIN, G. M., FAIRBAIRN, C. G. & COWEN, P. J. (1987*a*) The effects of dieting and weight loss on neuroendocrine responses to L-tryptophan, clonidine and apomorphine in volunteers: important implications for neuroendocrine investigation in depression. *Archives of General Psychiatry*, **44**, 952.

GRAY, G. (1971) *The Psychology of Fear and Stress*. London: Weidenfel and Nicolson.

GUDELSKY, G. A., KOENIG, J. I. & MELTZER, H. Y. (1986) Thermoregulatory responses to serotonin (5HT) receptor stimulation in the rat: evidence for opposing roles of $5HT_2$ and 5HT1A receptors. *Neuropharmacology*, **25**, 1307–1313.

HARRISON-READ, P. E. (1983) 'Wet dog shake' behaviour in rats may reflect functionally-opposed indoleaminergic systems involving different 5HT receptors. *British Journal of Pharmacology*, **78**, 92p.

HEAL, D. J., PHILPOT, K., MOLYNEUX, S. G., *et al* (1985) Intracerebroventricular administration of 5, 7-dihydroxytryptamine to mice increases both head-twitch responses and the number of cortical $5HT_2$ receptors. *Neuropharmacology*, **24**, 1201–1205.

HENINGER, G. R., CHARNEY, D. S. & STERNBERGE, D. E. (1984) Serotonergic function in depression. *Archives of General Psychiatry*, **41**, 398–402.

JOHNSTONE, E. C., CUNNINGHAM OWENS, D. G., FRITH, C. D., *et al* (1980) Neurotic illness and its response to anxiolytic and antidepressant treatment. *Psychological Medicine*, **10**, 321–328.

KAHN, R. J., MCNAIR, M., LIPMAN, S. R., *et al* (1986) Imipramine and chlordiazepoxide in depressive and anxiety disorders. *Archives of General Psychiatry*, **43**, 79–84.

KENNETT, G. A., DICKINSON, S. & CURZON, G. (1985) Enhancement of some 5-HT-dependent behavioural responses following repeated immobilization in rats. *Brain Research*, **330**, 253–263.

KENNETT, G. A., DOURISH, C. T. & CURZON, G. (1987) Antidepressant-like action of 5HT1A agonists and conventional antidepressants in an animal model of depression. *European Journal of Pharmacology*, **134**, 265–274.

KLEIN, D. F. (1964) Delineation of two drug-responsive anxiety symptoms. *Psychopharmacologia*, **5**, 397–408.

LAKOSKI, J. M. & AGHAJANIAN, G. K. (1985) Effects of ketanserin on neuronal responses to serotonin in the prefrontal cortex, lateral geniculate and dorsal raphe nucleus. *Neuropsychopharmacology*, **25**, 265–273.

LEYSEN, J. E., VAN GOMPEL, P., GOMMEREN, W., *et al* (1986) Down regulation of serotonin-S2 receptor sites in rat brain by chronic treatment with the serotonin-S2 antagonist: ritanserin and setoperone. *Psychopharmacology*, **88**, 434–444.

LEYSEN, J. E., VAN GOMPEL, P., VERWIMP, M., *et al* (1983) Role and localization of serotonin 2 (S2)-receptor-binding sites: effects of neuronal lesions. In *Molecular Pharmacology to Behavior* (eds P. Mandel & F. V. Defeudis). New York: Raven Press.

MASON, R. (1985) Characterisation of 5HT sensitive neurones in the rat CNS using ionophoresed 8-0-H-DPAT and ketanserin. *British Journal of Pharmacology*, **86**, 433p.

MELTZER, H. Y., PERLINE, R., TRICOU, B. J., *et al* (1984) Effect of 5-hydroxytryptophan on serum cortisol levels in major affective disorders: 1. Enhanced response in depression and mania. *Archives of General Psychiatry*, **41**, 366–374.

NAGAYAMA, H., HINGTEN, J. N. & APRISON, M. H. (1981) Postsynaptic action for four antidepressive drugs in an animal model of depression. *Pharmacology, Biochemistry and Behaviour*, **15**, 215–230.

NORTON, K. R. W., SIRELING, L. I., BHAT, A. V., *et al* (1984) A double-blind comparison of fluvoxamine, imipramine and placebo in depressed patients. *Journal of Affective Disorders*, **7**, 297–308.

PEROUTKA, S. J. & SNYDER, S. H. (1980) Long-term antidepressant treatment decreases spiroperidol-labelled serotonin receptor binding. *Science*, **210**, 88–90.

PETTY, F. & SHERMAN, A. D. (1983) Learned helplessness induction decreases *in vivo* cortical serotonin release. *Pharmacology, Biochemistry and Behaviour*, **18**, 649–650.

QUIK, M. & AZMITIA, E. (1983) Selective destruction of the serotonergic fibers of the fornix-fimbria and cingulum bundle increases $5HT_1$ but not $5HT_2$ receptors in rat midbrain. *European Journal of Pharmacology*, **90**, 377–384.

RICKELS, K., FEIGHNER, J. P. & SMITH, W. T. (1985) Alprazolam, amitriptyline, doxepin and placebo in the treatment of depression. *Archives of General Psychiatry*, **42**, 134–141.

SCHILDKRAUT, J. (1965) The catecholamine hypothesis of affective disorders: a review of supporting evidence. *American Journal of Psychiatry*, **112**, 509–522.

SHERMAN, A. D. & PETTY, F. (1980) Neurochemical basis of the action of antidepressants on learned helplessness. *Behavioral and Neural Biology*, **30**, 119–134.

SHERMAN, A. D. & PETTY, F. (1982) Additivity of neurochemical changes in learned helplessness and imipramine. *Behavioral and Neural Biology*, **35**, 344–353.

SIEVER, L. J., MURPHY, D. L., SLATER, S., *et al* (1984) Plasma prolactin changes following fenfluramine in depressed patients compared to controls: an evaluation of central serotonergic responsivity in depression. *Life Science*, **34**, 1029–1039.

SJOSTROM, R. & ROOS, B. E. (1972) 5-hydroxyindoleacetic acid and homovanillic acid in cerebrospinal fluid in manic-depressive psychosis. *European Journal of Clinical Pharmacology*, **4**, 170–176.

SOUBRIE, P., MARTIN, P., EL MESTIKAWY, S., *et al* (1986) The lesion of serotonergic neurons does not prevent antidepressant-induced reversal of escape failures produced by inescapable shocks in rats. *Pharmacology, Biochemistry and Behaviour*, **25**, 1–6.

STANLEY, M. & MANN, J. J. (1983) Increased serotonin-2 binding sites in frontal cortex of suicide victims. *Lancet*, *i*, 214–216.

STEIN, L. (1962) Effects and interactions of imipramine, chlorpromazine, reserpine and amphetamine on self-stimulation: possible neurophysiological basis of depression. In *Recent Advances in Biological Psychiatry IV* (ed. J. Wortis), pp. 208–288. New York: Plenum.

TRICKLEBANK, M. D., HUTSON, P. H. & CURZON, G. (1984) Analgesia induced by brief or more prolonged stress differs in its dependency on naloxone, 5-hydroxytryptamine and previous testing of analgesia. *Neuropharmacology*, **23**, 417–421.

TYE, N. C., EVERITT, B. J. & IVERSEN, S. D. (1977) 5-hydroxytryptamine and punishment. *Nature*, **268**, 741–743.

VETALANI, J., LEBRECHT, U. & PILC, A. (1981) Enhancement of responsiveness of the central serotonergic system and serotonin-2 receptor density in rat frontal cortex by electroconvulsive treatment. *European Journal of Pharmacology*, **76**, 81–85.

WEISS, S., SEBBEN, M., KEMP, D. E., *et al* (1986) Serotonin $5\text{-}HT_1$ receptors mediate inhibition of cyclic AMP production in neurons. *European Journal of Pharmacology*, **120**, 227–230.

Wilson, C. A. & Hunter, A. J. (1985) Progesterone stimulates sexual behaviour in female rats by increasing 5HT activity on $5HT_2$ receptors. *Brain Research*, **333**, 223-229.

Wise, C. D., Berger, B. D. & Stein, L. (1970) Serotonin: a possible mediator of behavioural suppression induced by anxiety. *Disorders of the Nervous System GWAN* (suppl. 31), 34-37.

9 Epidemiological observations on the concept of dysthymic disorder

D. P. GOLDBERG and K. W. BRIDGES

Dysthymic disorder is a new plastic box for some rather old wine. We would like to remind you about the wine and invite a consideration of the various containers that have been used until recently, and which are to be used in the future. Six related points are considered. First, to remind the reader of the taxonomic system with which we are all most familiar and describe this on a taxonomic grid, with one axis representing various combinations of anxious or depressive symptoms, and the other ranging from transient disorders to chronic disorders. Second, to remind the reader of what has been learned about the taxonomic predecessor of dysthymic disorder, which has been referred to as 'chronic neurosis'. Third, to present some findings from recent epidemiological surveys that have attempted to measure the prevalence of dysthymic disorder in community settings. Fourth, to show how the concept of dysthymic disorder compares with other related constructs in the taxonomic space generated by latent trait analysis. Fifth, to document the recent changes in classificatory rules of DSM-III-R (American Psychiatric Association, 1987) and ICD-10 (World Health Organization, 1988) in order to draw attention to the relationships between systems old and new. Finally, to argue that dysthymic disorder is a poorly defined construct representing a failure to achieve full restitution of symptoms of minor mood disorder over prolonged periods: it should almost certainly attract non-pharmacological interventions from doctors.

Our present taxonomic system

The ICD-9 system (World Health Organization, 1978) allowed for two dimensions of mood disorders: transient versus established illness, and combinations of anxious and depressive symptoms. In the former category pure depressive reactions (309.0) were to be distinguished from "other emotions" (309.2), while in the latter pure anxiety states (300.0) were to be distinguished from "neurotic depression" (300.4), and users were

TABLE 9.1
Common mood disorders: British concepts up to ICD–9, including those of Shepherd et al *(1966)*

	Anxiety states	*Mixed anxiety/ depression*	*Depression*
	309.0 Adjustment reactions:		
Transient states	309.2 with disturbance of other emotions		309.0 brief depressive reaction
Acute illnesses	300.0 Anxiety states	300.4 Neurotic depression (includes mixed anxiety depression)	
Chronic disorders		Shepherd *et al*: "chronic neurosis"	

specifically told that mixed states of anxiety and depression were to be included with pure depressive reactions. The system is peculiar, but we have all got used to it, and it is shown as Table 9.1.

Chronic neurosis

Those who are familiar with disorders in primary care settings have long been aware that there is an important group of patients with long-standing symptoms of both anxiety and depression. The finding that a substantial proportion of mental illnesses seen in community settings have lasted over one year was firmly established in Shepherd *et al*'s (1966) classic epidemiological study in England, and was confirmed in the United States by Regier *et al* (1985). Regier *et al* have shown that chronic disorders (meaning those with a duration of greater than one year) account for five-sixths of the morbidity seen in a primary care setting in Wisconsin, and that the group with prolonged personality disorder constituted the highest proportion of the total population with severe disability. Only a third of those with severe disability had psychotic disorders: the remainder received diagnoses of affective illness, anxiety disorders, substance abuse and "prolonged disorders".

Cooper's work on the General Practice Research Unit (1972*a*,*b*) showed how psychiatric disorders seen in primary care settings could be divided into two broad groups: acute disorders, which were most usually in association with stressful life events, and chronic disorders, which were strongly associated with long-standing social problems. An intervention study using a controlled design showed that attached social workers resulted in significant gains for both the clinical and social adjustment of these patients (Cooper *et al*, 1975), while a more detailed account of the actual social interventions offered (Shepherd *et al*, 1979) stressed the frequency of relatively mundane practical tasks such as co-ordinating services and disseminating information in the actual work carried out with these patients. The latter study also

TABLE 9.2
Common mood disorders: DSM–III system

	Anxiety states	*Mixed anxiety/ depression*	*Depression*
		309.00 Adjustment disorders:	
Transient states	309.24 with anxiety	309.28 with mixed emotions	309.00 with depression
Acute illnesses	300.01 Panic disorder 300.02 Generalised anxiety disorder	296.2x Major depressive episode	
Chronic disorders		300.40 Dysthymic disorder	

showed that there was no relationship between the amount of contact with the social worker and outcome: indeed, those in continuous contact were often "unchanged or worse" when seen by independent researchers at follow-up. At the time that these studies were carried out the DSM–III system (American Psychiatric Association, 1980) did not exist: however, as a research worker on the unit at the time, one of the present authors can confirm that the majority of the patients would have received a diagnosis of dysthymic disorder, major depressive episode or generalised anxiety disorder. There was no tendency whatever for these patients to separate into natural clinical groupings: the typical patient had a 'pan-neurosis', with symptoms of anxiety, depression, poor sleep, fatigue, and irritability, most often with somatic symptoms. Such patients received fairly intensive psychotropic medication from primary care physicians, but those with intractable social problems maintained their symptoms at follow-up despite such medication. However, in the controlled trial of social intervention those receiving the intervention consumed on average 1.5 patient-months of medication less than controls treated by their family doctor alone, and yet still managed to do better.

A controlled study by Corney (1981) showed that, while social work intervention could not be shown to be effective for a group of women diagnosed as depressed in primary care settings, it was effective for that subgroup recorded as having "acute-on-chronic" onsets. Translated into the language of DSM–III, the latter group of patients would appear to correspond to dysthymic patients experiencing a major depressive episode.

The concept of dysthymic disorder, with some recent epidemiological findings

The DSM–III system is shown in Table 9.2: it is strikingly similar to the ICD system except that adjustment disorders have been tidied up somewhat, and Shepherd's "chronic neurosis" now comes into official existence, albeit by purloining the code used for neurotic depression in the rest of the world. Panic disorder, given a somewhat ambivalent reception in the UK (Gelder, 1989), squats cuckoo-like alongside "generalised anxiety disorder", but otherwise the chief innovations are the defined criteria for the various diagnoses.

Three recent surveys have attempted to estimate the prevalence of dysthymic disorder using these criteria. A large community survey by Newman *et al* (1989) in Alberta gives a lifetime prevalence of dysthymic disorder of 4.5%, to be compared with a one-month prevalence of 2.6% for major depressive episode, and of 14.5% for any DSM–III-diagnosable disorder.

von Korff *et al* (1987) have also chosen to estimate lifetime prevalence of dysthymic disorder among those attending primary care physicians in Baltimore: here dysthymic disorder appears in 3.7% of attenders, to be compared with a one-month prevalence of 25% for any DSM–III disorder. The higher one-month prevalence for "any disorder" was to be expected in a survey of clinic attenders; the somewhat lower figure for lifetime prevalence of dysthymic disorder is unexpected (but then the whole concept of 'lifetime prevalence' fills any European epidemiologist with existential dread).

The present authors (Goldberg & Bridges, 1987) have estimated the point prevalence of dysthymic disorder among consecutive inceptions of illness in primary care settings in Greater Manchester as 3.1%, to be compared with a prevalence of 33.2% for any DSM–III disorder.

Despite the use of 'lifetime prevalence' it is of interest that most of the cases of dysthymic disorder mentioned in the three surveys are picked up by the General Health Questionnaire (Goldberg, 1972) (52.3%, 75.3% and 90.9% respectively), indicating the tendency of such patients to continue to report symptoms at the time of the survey.

Dysthymic disorder and latent trait analysis

The 11 cases of dysthymic disorder seen in the Manchester survey were included in a study by Grayson *et al* (1987) which was concerned to compare diagnostic concepts using latent trait analysis. The interested reader is referred to introductory papers by Duncan-Jones *et al* (1968) and to the paper describing the use of latent-trait analysis to generate a two-dimensional symptom space using the same data (Goldberg *et al*, 1987).

It is possible to enter diagnoses into the latent-trait analysis in much the same way as symptoms, since each member of the population can be said to possess, or not to possess, the diagnosis under consideration. For each diagnosis, we can then consider three variables: the slope, which is a measure of how well the diagnosis discriminates between subjects at its point of optimal discrimination in bivariate space; the direction, which indicates to what extent the diagnosis is measuring the anxiety symptom dimension, and to what extent the depression dimension; and the threshold, which measures the severity of the diagnosis, compared with other diagnoses.

Briefly, the salient point about dysthymic disorder is that it has a very poor slope indeed, indicating that it is not discriminating at all well between subjects. In fact, it is easily the worst of some 15 diagnostic concepts considered in this very important respect. It may be that with a larger group of patients with the disorder things would improve, but the present results confirm the wisdom of Dr Spitzer and his colleagues in re-evaluating their Research Diagnostic Criteria.

It would indeed have been very surprising had dysthymic disorder turned out to be a satisfactory concept, since in order to qualify for the diagnosis one needed any three from a check-list of no fewer than 13 symptoms. It is a matter of simple arithmetic to calculate that there are 1716 different combinations of three items from a list of 13, and thus there are that many routes to the same diagnosis: small wonder that the slope of the concept is so poor.

DSM-III-R, ICD-10, and all that

In DSM-III-R one must have at least one from a list of six symptoms to qualify for the diagnosis of dysthymic disorder, so the concept is about 286 times as good as it was. It needed to be. The list of symptoms is now more focused upon depression—this is also welcome, since the direction of the previous concept was very close indeed to the anxiety axis. One is now allowed to have periods of normality for up to three months, whereas the old rules only allowed "a few months". Thus, the concept is milder, and shifted towards depression.

The complete changes are shown as Table 9.3. The cuckoo has indeed pushed generalised anxiety disorder from its nest, so that raters now have a choice between a chronic, mild anxiety disorder and a chronic, mild depressive disorder. The fact that the patients themselves do not remotely correspond to this neat dichotomy is probably of no concern to the taxonomists.

At the World Health Organization, ICD classifications are also being nervously altered in ways reminiscent of, but by no means identical with, the changes to DSM-III. The international team is uneasily aware that only a quantitative distinction can be made between psychotic forms of depressive illness and minor forms, so that the picture now begins to look more complicated: it is shown in Table 9.4.

From the authors' standpoint the major innovation here is an interesting one: mixed anxiety/depression is now allowed, but is considered to be an anxiety disorder. We do not know what data informed this decision, but

TABLE 9.3
Common mood disorders: DSM–III–R system

	Anxiety states	*Mixed anxiety/ depression*	*Depression*
		309 Adjustment disorders:	
Transient states	309.24 with anxiety	309.28 with mixed emotions	309.04 with depression
Acute illnesses	300.01 Panic disorder	296.2x Major depressive episode	
Chronic disorders	300.02 Generalised anxiety disorder (milder; chronic)		300.04 Dysthymic disorder (milder, purer depression)

TABLE 9.4
Common mood disorders: ICD–10 system

	Anxiety only	*Anxious + depressed*	*Depressed only (mild)*	*Depressed only (severe)*
		F43.2 Adjustment disorders		
Transient	F43.22 with disturbance of other emotions		F43.20 with depression	
Acute	F.41.0 Panic disorder	F.41.2 Mixed anxiety depression	F.31.1 Mild depressive episode	F.31.0 Severe depressive episode
Chronic	F.41.1 Generalised anxiety disorder (tends to be chronic)	F.34.1 Dysthymic disorder (very mild)	F.33.1 Mild recurrent depressive disorder	F.33.0 Recurrent severe depressive disorder

it does seem to make sense in terms of the syndromes with which we have been most familiar in our primary care research. It is difficult to know quite where to put dysthymic disorder in the new ICD classification, since the place it seems to occupy in DSM–III–R has been usurped by recurrent depressive disorder—which can itself be either mild or severe. So, presumably it is in some intermediate place, as shown in Table 9.4.

The doubt over this classification is whether we need quite so many categories. However, it will probably take about a decade to gather enough data with a new classification to see whether such myriad subdivisions are heuristically useful, and this will keep many research teams harmlessly occupied.

Conclusions

There can be no doubt that it was right to produce a concept of chronic disorder, and equally no doubt that the first attempt, dysthymic disorder according to its original definition, was seriously flawed. Thus, we applaud the concept, and welcome the revised version.

Whatever we adopt as working clinicians for our everyday taxonomy, it is important that our new taxonomies do not prevent us from asking ourselves about the nature of the problem. As research constructs, both the major systems leave a great deal to be desired, in that they do not encourage us to ask ourselves questions about the nature of morbidity. Neither of the new taxonomies corresponds to natural groupings among the patients, yet either will encourage the unthinking investigator to suppose that open questions have been answered.

Another hazard of medicalising what seems to be a mild inability to normalise in the face of unremitting social problems is that the unfortunate patients may be given drugs. Clinicians should remember what we know about chronic neurosis, and see that those with chronic social problems receive appropriate social help, and that we consider non-pharmacological ways of normalising (relaxation therapy, restoring sleep and taking exercise; and decreasing inappropriate use of alcohol, tobacco and drugs that cannot possibly normalise the patient). These patients are often physically ill and taking drugs for hypertension or arthritis, and they are often poor. We should not be using concepts that encourage doctors to prescribe additional drugs that are often ineffective, expensive, and prone to produce interactive side-effects with more essential drugs.

To finish on a more optimistic note, the main advantage of the concept that we foresee is that it is likely to encourage more research into the movement of vulnerable individuals between subclinical states (such as dysthymic disorder) and more severe depressive disorders. Our available data suggest that there is considerable movement between these categories, and knowledge may advance if we improve our understanding of the natural history of the common mood disorders.

Symposium discussion

DR HIRSCHFELD: Professor Goldberg, do you think that there are patients with mild chronic depressions who would respond to drug therapy, and if so, how would you identify them?

PROFESSOR GOLDBERG: I think the question you pose is a good one. I learned a great deal from Dr Akiskal's talk indicating that there was a subgroup among his dysthymic disorders that appeared to benefit from drugs. I am quite happy to give people anything, including drug interventions, that can be shown to help them. What upsets me is that my colleagues, once they get the armament of drugs in their hands, tend not to put the weapon down very easily, and they will go on hitting the patient with it even when all chance is lost of actually helping affairs by prescribing. That is my anxiety.

I certainly do not wish to stop research. I have no doubt at all that the new DSM–III–R concept, which is, as I have said, a better concept of minor depression, will lead to the delineation of subgroups that may benefit from antidepressants—not a benzodiazepine. That is to be welcomed, and of course I applaud it. But one of the things that has become very clear to me, listening to the excellent presentations from the USA, is that the kind of patients that get trapped by one of your classifications in consulting settings are just not the same as the people we see in our primary-care settings. I think that, whatever the concept means to consulting psychiatrists, to me, in primary-care research, the concept, if it is a useful one, is about the states that are left after a depressive episode finishes and the states which sometimes chronically usher in and indicate people as being vulnerable to developing major depressive episodes under stress. Clearly, special studies have to be done in that setting, without trying to generalise the rules that are produced in some consulting setting and thinking they will necessarily apply to the other.

References

AMERICAN PSYCHIATRIC ASSOCIATION (1980) *Diagnostic and Statistical Manual of Mental Disorders* (3rd edn) (DSM-III). Washington, DC: APA.

—— (1987) *Diagnostic and Statistical Manual of Mental Disorders* (3rd edn, revised) (DSM-III-R). Washington, DC: APA.

COOPER, B. (1972*a*) Clinical and social aspects of chronic neurosis. *Proceedings of the Royal Society of Medicine*, **65**, 509–512.

—— (1972*b*) Social correlates of psychiatric illness in the community. In *Approaches to Action* (ed. G. MacLachlan), pp. 65–70. Oxford: Oxford University Press.

——, HARWIN, B. G., DEPLA, C., *et al* (1975) Mental care in the community: an evaluative study. *Psychological Medicine*, **5**, 372–380.

CORNEY, R. (1981) Social work effectiveness in the management of depressed women: a clinical trial. *Psychological Medicine*, **11**, 417–424.

DUNCAN-JONES, P., GRAYSON, D. & MORAN, P. (1986) The utility of latent trait analysis in psychiatric epidemiology. *Psychological Medicine*, **16**, 391–405.

GELDER, M. (1989) Panic disorder: fact or fiction? *Psychological Medicine*, **19**, 277–284.

GOLDBERG, D. P. (1972) *The Detection of Psychiatric Illness by Questionnaire*. London: Oxford University Press.

—— & BRIDGES, K. (1987) Screening for psychiatric illness in general practice: the general practitioner versus the screening questionnaire. *Journal of the Royal College of General Practitioners*, **37**, 15–18.

——, ——, DUNCAN-JONES, P., *et al* (1987) Dimensions of neurosis seen in primary care settings. *Psychological Medicine*, **7**, 461–470.

GRAYSON, D., BRIDGES, K., DUNCAN-JONES, P., *et al* (1987) The relationship between symptoms and diagnosis of minor psychiatric disorder in general practice. *Psychological Medicine*, **17**, 933–942.

NEWMAN, S., BLAND, R. & ORN, H. (1989) The General Health Questionnaire as a screening instrument in a community survey. *Psychological Medicine*, **19**, (in press).

REGIER, D. A., BURKE, J. D., MANDERSCHEID, R. W., *et al* (1985) The chronic mentally ill in primary care. *Psychological Medicine*, **15**, 266–273.

SHEPHERD, M., COOPER, B., BROWN, A. C. *et al* (1966) *Psychiatric Illness in General Practice*. Oxford: Oxford University Press.

——, HARWIN, B. G., DEPLA, C., *et al* (1979) Social work and the primary care of mental disorder. *Psychological Medicine*, **9**, 661–669.

VON KORFF, M., SHAPIRO, S., BURKE, J., *et al* (1987) Anxiety and depression in a primary care clinic: comparison of DIS, GHQ and general practitioner assessments. *Archives of General Psychiatry*, **44**, 152–156.

WORLD HEALTH ORGANIZATION (1978) *Mental Disorders: Glossary and Guide to their Classification in Accordance with the Ninth Revision of the International Classification of Diseases* (ICD-9). Geneva: WHO.

—— (1988) *International Classification of Diseases, Draft of Chapter V*. (ICD-10). Geneva: WHO.

10 Dysthymia: a clinician's perspective

Z. RIHMER

Not all mild, chronic depressions are primary in origin. Regarding the new concept of dysthymic disorder, it is a heterogeneous group of mild, mainly chronic depressions of various aetiologies, and its delineated subgroups need different treatment strategies. While the affective component in chronic secondary depressions and in character spectrum depression is not primary in origin, the dysthymic residuum of primary unipolar depression and subaffective dysthymia does belong to the primary affective spectrum (Akiskal, 1983).

The author's clinical experiences, as well as case histories, are presented to illustrate the definitely clinical usefulness of this new concept, which helps discriminate different subgroups of patients who respond to different treatments. This concept also suggests that psychiatrists must give up the traditional stereotype in their diagnostic thinking, that is, that 'mild' symptoms automatically indicates neurosis or personality disturbances. The clinical diagnosis has to be based on a special constellation of familial/genetic, developmental, phenomenological, and biological data, rather than on illness severity alone. For this reason, clinicians must understand and use research findings and related new concepts that can improve their diagnostic ability, reducing treatment failures.

In the last two decades depressive disorders have gained increasing attention, and treatment of them has undergone a major shift. However, unfavourable (chronic) course (Keller *et al*, 1983) and drug resistance can often occur in various forms of depression, although not in equal distribution: secondary depressives more frequently show chronic course and drug resistance than patients with primary depression (Akiskal, 1982). Among the strategies that show promise in the selection of the best treatments, the first and most important is correct clinical diagnosis. This is relatively easy when the clinical picture is 'typical', that is, severe enough to identify it with the textbook descriptions. Diagnostic dilemma occurs mostly in extremely severe and in mild cases.

As a full-time clinical psychiatrist who has been working nearly 20 years at an in-patient department for acute admissions, I summarise in this chapter the usefulness of the new concept of dysthymic disorder (Akiskal, 1983). Since our group has published some clinically orientated investigations in this field, in the first part of this chapter I also briefly review the clinical research literature from the perspective of everyday practice.

Nosological and research considerations

It is generally accepted that the classic manifestation of primary affective disorder exists in two main forms: unipolar and bipolar depression (Fieve & Dunner, 1975; Andreasen, 1982). However, more recent findings support the need for further subclassification of bipolar illness into bipolar I and bipolar II subgroups (Fieve & Dunner, 1975; Rihmer *et al*, 1982), and of unipolar depression into familial, sporadic and depressive spectrum subtypes (Winokur *et al*, 1978; Andreasen, 1982). By now it is also well established that psychotic features (delusions, hallucinations, catatonic symptoms) may occur in primary depression and mania, representing the psychotic forms of the primary affective illness (Abrams & Taylor, 1976; Pope & Lipinski, 1978; Kendell, 1985).

In contrast to our earlier practice, more and more attention is now paid to the milder mood disorders occurring in ambulatory psychiatric settings, and in non-psychiatric departments. 'Neurotic depression', including diagnoses of Research Diagnostic Criteria (RDC) minor depression (Spitzer *et al*, 1978) and dysthymic disorder (DSM–III; American Psychiatric Association, 1980) are some of the most frequent psychiatric diagnoses both in the community (Weissman & Myers, 1978; Blazer *et al*, 1985) and in primary care (von Korff *et al*, 1987).

Contrary to primary depression with a 'typical' clinical picture, until the last few years there had been little consensus about the nature and specificity of treatment of these mild depressive states. Clinicians who believe that 'neurotic depression' has psychosocial and psychodynamic aetiology prefer psychotherapy and anxiolytics, while others who consider this category as a mild form of primary affective illness are more prone to use the same drugs as are generally accepted in the treatment of classic depressions.

Significant state-dependent personality changes have been reported in mania and also in primary depression (Hirschfeld & Klerman, 1979; Liebowitz *et al*, 1979). The interaction of personality and illness, and accentuation of personality traits during the low-grade depressive states, may give a 'neurotic' or 'psychopathic' mask to the underlying affective disorder. Prevalent misdiagnoses in such cases are 'neurotic depression', 'personality disorder' (mostly borderline type), and, when the patients report stressful life events, the diagnosis of 'reactive depression' is often made (Akiskal *et al*, 1978; Akiskal, 1981). Such misdiagnosed patients are generally inadequately treated, resulting in chronic course (Weissman & Klerman, 1977; Schatzberg & Cole, 1978). However, life events preceding the onset have been reported in a substantial proportion of patients with unipolar and bipolar depression (Lloyd, 1980), and with mania (Ambelas, 1987). Since life events play a precipitating, rather than a causative role in the development of primary depression and mania (Lloyd, 1980; Ambelas, 1987), although they are sometimes epiphenomenal, the significance of life events should not be overemphasised.

A substantial overlap exists between the terms 'neurotic depression' and 'atypical depression'. This latter group is characterised by mild intensity, early onset, predominance of women, and good response to monoamine oxidase inhibitors. Subtype A presents marked anxiety, hysterical and phobic features, while subtype B shows predominance of reversed vegetative symptoms, often accompanied by lability of mood, and chronic pain (Davidson *et al*, 1982, 1985).

While primary major affective disorders are heterogeneous illnesses as regards their genetics, polarity, biochemistry, etc. (Fieve & Dunner, 1975; Andreasen, 1982), the low-grade depressive states which may be either primary or non-primary are even more heterogeneous.

The heterogeneity of mild, chronic or intermittent depressive states was demonstrated by Akiskal *et al*. Based on family history, phenomenology, natural course, and drug response, it was found that cyclothymic disorder was a subaffective or attenuated form, and mostly the precursor of bipolar major affective illness (Akiskal *et al*, 1977). Similar results were published by Depue *et al* (1981). Investigating the course of the illness of 100 patients with 'neurotic depression', Akiskal *et al* (1978) found that at three- to four-year follow-up 18% developed bipolar (mostly bipolar II) and 22% unipolar major depression, many of them with endogenous features. This is consistent with earlier observations (Paskind, 1930; Watts, 1957) and the results of Stone (1978). Bronisch *et al* (1985) also reported that six (12%) out of their 50 index patients with 'neurotic depression' had committed suicide, 22 (44%) fulfilled the RDC for primary major depression, and two (4%) for bipolar disorder over a seven-year follow-up. The relationship between endogenous and 'neurotic depression' is supported by the study of Eastwood & Stiasny (1978), showing a significant seasonal variation in both groups in spring and autumn. No other diagnoses overall showed seasonality, although personality disorders and drug addiction (particularly in young persons) exhibited similar trends.

In our previous study we found the same high rate of good response to sleep deprivation, and hypomanias at follow-up in patients with primary major and minor depression, but not in patients with secondary depression (Rihmer & Szucs, 1979). In a retrospective study of 72 manic–depressive female in-patients (50 bipolar I and 22 bipolar II) we found that in 60 patients the illness began with a depressive phase. In 20 out these 60 (33%) the first hospital diagnosis was 'neurotic or reactive depression' (Rihmer, unpublished). In a later study we investigated the dexamethasone suppression test (DST), family history, response to thymoleptics, and short-term course in 16 patients with 'masked depression' (definite RDC minor depression *and* predominant somatic complaints). Twelve patients showed abnormal DST, three had a positive family history of primary affective illness in first-degree relatives, 11 responded well to antidepressants, and three showed definite (pharmacologically mobilised) hypomania during the follow-up (Rihmer *et al*, 1983). This indicates that the majority of cases of RDC minor depression plus somatic masking may be a mild, subaffective variant of primary major depression of either unipolar or bipolar type.

However, not all mild, chronic depressions are primary in origin. Chronic depressions are a heterogeneous group of depressive illnesses with various ages of onset, and various familial/genetic, developmental, and medical histories. The new concept of dysthymic disorder (Akiskal, 1983) is based on the following subclassification: (a) late-onset primary unipolar depression with residual chronicity, (b) chronic depression secondary to non-affective psychiatric or incapitating medical diseases, and (c) characterological depressions with early onset. This latter group includes: (a) thymoleptic and lithium non-responsive character spectrum depression, which corresponds closely to Winokur's depression spectrum disease group (Winokur *et al*, 1978), and (b) subaffective dysthymic disorders which are the subsyndromal manifestations of primary major (unipolar and bipolar) affective illness, which respond as well to thymoleptics and to lithium as do 'ordinary' depressions (Akiskal *et al*, 1980, 1981).

The subclassification of characterological depressions into two further subtypes is also supported by our study (Szadoczky *et al*, 1983). We investigated the DST and response to tricyclic antidepressants in 33 in-patients with DSM–III dysthymic disorder. The patients were subdivided into subaffective dysthymics ($n = 20$) and character spectrum depressives ($n = 13$), based on pre-treatment clinical data (onset, course, personality, developmental and family history) as defined by Akiskal *et al* (1980). Thirteen patients (65%) with subaffective dysthymia, but none with character spectrum depressions, showed abnormal DST results. This 65% rate is the same figure as found by us in 93 in-patients with primary major, unipolar and bipolar depression (Rihmer *et al*, 1984). As for the drug response, among subaffective dysthymics there were 11 responders (including two hypomanic switches), six partial responders, and three non-responders. In contrast, in the character spectrum group, there were no responders, only three partial responders, and ten non-responders.

Schatzberg *et al* (1983) and Roy *et al* (1985), on the other hand, reported substantially lower rates of abnormal DST (16% and 18% respectively) in patients with DSM–III dysthymic disorder, but both studies consisted of a heterogeneous group of patients without any distinction between subaffective (primary) dysthymia and character spectrum (non-primary) depression. In addition, Schatzberg *et al* (1983) used only one, while we (Szadoczky *et al*, 1983) collected two post-dexamethasone blood samples.

The clinical consequence of studies reviewed above is that the precise definition of DSM–III dysthymic disorder, as well as the poorly defined

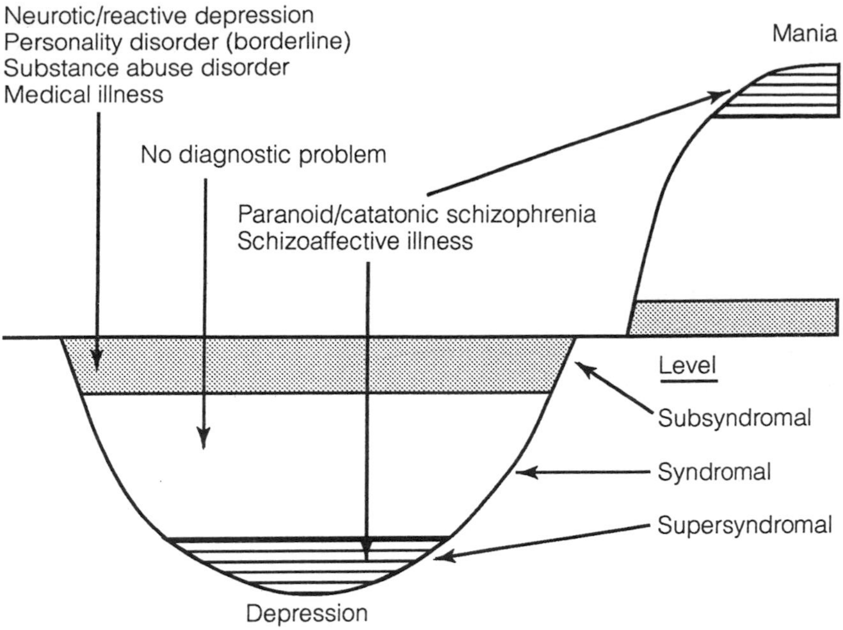

Fig. 10.1. Different levels of severity and the most frequent misdiagnoses in primary affective illness

diagnoses of 'neurotic', or 'reactive' depression are too broad, since they contain various groups of depressions with different aetiologies and treatment responses. Clinical diagnoses, mentioned above, should never be made or accepted without criticism.

The clinician and the dysthymic patient

While patients with acute major depression are generally referred to in- or out-patient units because of the sudden appearance of symptoms, chronic low-grade depressives are usually seen by psychiatrists and by other professionals because of complications (alcohol and drug abuse, suicide attempt, delirium, etc.). The psychiatrists are often under an obligation to treat patients before the final clinical diagnosis is established.

According to my clinical experience, diagnostic problems in affective disorders occur most frequently as a result of the confusion of severity with aetiology. Severity and aetiology are two absolutely independent dimensions, and unfortunately many clinicians believe they are related. Figure 10.1 shows a diagram of an idealised manic–depressive (bipolar I) illness. Three ranges of severity are delineated. If the low severity range is called 'subsyndromal', the most severe (i.e. psychotic) level could be called 'supersyndromal'.

The danger of misdiagnosis is most common at sub- or supersyndromal levels, while generally no diagnostic dilemma occurs in the 'syndromal' range.

Returning to the clinical aspects of low-grade, chronic depressions, the subclassification of dysthymic disorders seems to be useful in discriminating between different groups of patients who need different treatment strategies.

Diagnostic aspects of dysthymic disorders

(a) The first step is the delineation of chronic depressions secondary to non-affective psychiatric or incapacitating medical disorders. Careful medical and psychiatric examination (including past history) may help this distinction. However, one person may have two or more illnesses, and many depressed patients (especially in old age) have concomitant medical illness(es). This may sometimes be epiphenomenal, or only interact with the primary affective disorder. On the other hand, somatic symptoms frequently mask the underlying depression (Kielholz, 1973; Rihmer *et al*, 1983). The affective origin in such cases often remains unrecognised, and diagnosis of physical illness is stated. The distinction between the (i) *causative*, (ii) *epiphenomenal*, and (iii) *masking* nature of somatic symptoms is one of the most exciting issues in psychiatric practice. If the determination of the causative role of a given medical or non-affective psychiatric disorder remains unsuccessful, adequate antidepressant pharmacotherapy may be helpful, if it is not contraindicated. The observation of the patients' reaction on one or two sleep deprivations can also give valuable information (Rihmer & Szucs, 1979).

(b) The second step is the careful examination of past history to establish or exclude the possibility that the present state is a residuum of a late-onset primary unipolar (or sometimes bipolar II) depression. If this is the case, the patient may need vigorous antidepressant pharmacotherapy.

(c) If the clinician can exclude the above-mentioned two versions, it is very possible that the patient has characterological depression, especially when this condition began early in life with insidious onset. However, this group is also heterogeneous. Many patients belong to the primary affective spectrum (subaffective dysthymia, subunipolar or sub-bipolar type) and they need the same treatment strategy as primary depressives, while others belong to the character pathology (character spectrum disorder). The patients of this latter group are non-responsive to thymoleptic and lithium treatment, and they need various forms of psychotherapy, family counselling, and sometimes low-dosage neuroleptics.

The cross-sectional picture is of low-grade chronic depressions, and particularly in characterological depressions may be quite similar. When it shows only few features (diurnal and seasonal variation, hypersomnic/retarded picture, marked obsessionality), that may be a guide to differential diagnosis, collection of further data about family members, pre-morbid development, and past history (including drug history) is very important.

TABLE 10.1
The broad concept of masked depression

Subtype	*Level of masking*	*Source of masking*	*Clinical consequences*
Masked I	Biological	Underlying illness, or interaction of personality and illness	Somatic masking: masked depression[1] psychogenic pain syndrome[2] atypical depression, V-type[2] Psychic masking: atypical depression, A-type[2] personality disorder
Masked II	Social	Patient (self-medication)	Substance abuse
Masked III	Educational	Doctor (misdiagnosis)	Inadequate treatment: anxiolytics, sedatives, sleeping pills, etc.

1. As defined by Kielholz (1973).
2. For details see Davidson *et al* (1982, 1985).

Family history of alcohol and drug abuse, or suicide not related to primary affective illness, sociopathy, broken home, onset in early adolescence, sociopathic personality traits, intermittent course (with rarely superimposed major depressive episodes) are highly indicative of character spectrum disorder. On the other hand, family history of unipolar or bipolar depression, loaded pedigree, normal childhood and developmental history, predominantly depressed (gloomy, pessimistic, self-critical, sceptical, etc.) personality features, which sometimes alternate with brief 'well', or 'active', 'optimistic' periods, good response to thymoleptics (Akiskal *et al*, 1980, 1981), and significant improvement with sleep deprivation (Rihmer & Szucs, 1979), strongly suggest the diagnosis of subaffective dysthymia.

Alcohol and drug abuse, which are frequent components of all types of affective disorders, are easy to recognise as complications at a syndromal level. However, at a subsyndromal level this complication may completely mask the underlying illness (Akiskal *et al*, 1977, 1978). A typical clinical presentation, primarily with anxious, phobic, or hysterical features (Davidson *et al*, 1982) which may or may not be the results of accentuation of pre-morbid personality traits can also mask the mild affective illness. An extreme version of the interaction of personality and disease can be seen in a proportion of patients with a DSM–III diagnosis of (non-schizotypal) borderline personality disorder. Several pieces of phenomenological, biological, and pharmacological evidence suggest that the majority of such patients really have dysthymic, cyclothymic, bipolar II, or schizoaffective illness (Akiskal, 1981; Baxter *et al*, 1984; McNamara *et al*, 1984; Akiskal *et al*, 1985*a*,*b*). It suggests that clinicians should not limit their attention only to the personality of patients with low-grade psychopathology. The equation of dysthymia with neurotic or personality disorders represents a special masking of the clinical picture by the clinician, resulting in repeated

TABLE 10.2

Some clinical and pharmacological characteristics of patients with subaffective dysthymic and character spectrum disorder

Subgroups	*Mean age of admission (years)*	*No. of patients with previous admissions (%)*	*Most frequent previous diagnoses*	*Drug response*[1]	*No. of patients with pharmacogenic hypomania (%)*
Subaffective dysthymia ($n = 37$)	39.7	20 (54)	Personality disorder Neurotic/reactive depression Substance abuse Cyclothymia	R 25 PR 5 NR 7	8 (22)
Character-spectrum disorder ($n = 40$)	37.2	20 (50)	Neurotic/reactive depression Personality disorder Substance abuse	R 3 PR 5 NR 15	2 (5)

1. The patients received one or two trials of imipramine (175–250 mg/day), amitriptyline (125–250 mg/day), maprotiline (150–225 mg/day), and/or nialamide (125–150 mg/day), either alone, or in combination with lithium and carbamazepine. Only 23 patients with character spectrum depression have completed one or two trials.
R = responders, PR = partial responders, NR = non-responders.

treatment failures. In my opinion, there are at least three levels and reasons for masking in depressive symptomatology. They are summarised in Table 10.1.

The analysis of pre-morbid personality has an important role in the separation of different subgroups of patients with dysthymic disorders.

Previously we reported that polyglottism (i.e. good ability to learn foreign languages by internal rather than external motivation) was significantly more frequent in bipolar patients than in unipolars, and than in the general population of Hungary (Rihmer, 1982). Polyglottism seems to be related to cyclothymic or hypomanic aspects of pre-morbid personality of bipolar patients. Our uncontrolled clinical observations suggest that polyglottism can be seen only in a small proportion of patients with characterological depression, but is highly concentrated among patients with subaffective dysthymia of the sub-bipolar type.

Dysthymic disorders in a psychiatric in-patient unit

The total number of admissions to our female in-patient department between 1 January 1984 and 31 December 1985 was 870, of whom 164 had chronic mild depression. There were 31 patients with chronic primary major depression (28 unipolar, 3 bipolar II), 56 patients with chronic secondary depression, and 77 patients with characterological depression as defined by Akiskal (1983). All characterological depressives met the DSM–III criteria of dysthymic disorder. Based on pre-treatment criteria (Akiskal, 1983), such as onset, course, personality, developmental and family history, there were 37 subaffective dysthymics, and 40 character spectrum depressives. A detailed analysis of the genetic, developmental, phenomenological, and neuroendocrinological aspects of the patients of these two subgroups is in progress. Some clinical findings are summarised in Table 10.2.

About half of the patients in both subgroups have had previous hospital admissions (generally at another in-patient department) and the most frequent previous diagnoses were 'neurotic' or 'reactive' depression, 'personality disorder', and 'alcohol or drug abuse'. All subaffective dysthymics and 23 out of the character spectrum depressives have completed one or two trials with thymoleptics (imipramine, amitriptyline, maprotiline, 125–250 mg/day, nialamide 125–150 mg/day) either alone, or in combination with lithium or carbamazepine. Subaffective dysthymics responded well (sometimes dramatically well), and several previously diagnosed 'neurotic' or 'reactive' depressions, 'personality disorders', and some 'hysterical neuroses' disappeared in a few weeks. Character spectrum depressives responded generally poorly to thymoleptics. Pharmacologically mobilised hypomanias were observed in 22% of subaffective dysthymics, and in 5% of character spectrum depressives (Table 10.2).

Our results are similar to those of Akiskal *et al* (1980, 1981), and support the clinical utility of the new concept of dysthymic disorder.

Illustrative case histories

Case 1

Mrs A is a 47-year-old married housewife, with unremarkable family and developmental history. Her personality was predominantly depressed and pessimistic. At age 42 Mrs A was admitted to a neurological department because of her headache, memory and concentration difficulties, mild insomnia, and anergia. Her somatic findings were negative, except the computerised tomography (CT) scan, which showed a middle-grade enlargement of ventricle III, and sulcal 'atrophy' at the frontal lobe region. Her illness was considered as cerebral atrophy, and she was treated 'symptomatically' (analgesics, sleeping pills, etc.). Her condition did not change, and she was readmitted six times during the following five years in the same department. She used more and more analgesics, and in May 1983 Mrs A was admitted to our in-patient department because of drug dependence. After three weeks of abstinence she was definitely dysthymic. The family members, including her older daughter, who was a university student in the faculty of psychology, did not want to believe that the patient was probably suffering from an easily treated affective illness. Nevertheless, Mrs A showed a significant improvement on amitriptyline (225 mg/day), and by the third week she became symptom free. She began working again, and at the follow-up in May 1989 she was absolutely well. Although she is not hypomanic, according to her family members "she is better than even before her illness".

This case vignette of the patient with subunipolar subaffective dysthymia illustrates that both the illness (headache, 'pseudodementia'), and the patient (through her drug abuse) can mask dysthymic disorder. However, the neurologist also assisted in the masking (misdiagnosis), not knowing that some patients with primary affective illness may have cerebral ventricular and sulcal enlargement without any evidence of organic (neurological) disease (Rieder *et al*, 1983).

Case 2

Ms B is a 23-year-old unmarried medical student who was referred to our out-patient department by another dysthymic patient who was successfully treated by us. The father of Ms B was a cyclothymic who had two major depressive episodes with retardation and hypersomnia, which remitted spontaneously within four months. The maternal grandfather was chronically hypomanic. Ms B has an extrovert, energic personality with mild cyclothymic features ('down and well periods' without any evidence of hypomania). She has a very good ability in foreign languages. At age 20 she gradually became retarded, pessimistic, anxious, and hypersomnic. She was seen as an out-patient by a psychiatrist who was not interested in her family history. The diagnosis of neurotic depression was made and Ms B was treated with anxiolytics. Her condition worsened, and she changed psychiatrist, but the diagnosis and treatment did not change. Ms B began to use alcohol, and stopped her studies at the university. At the first visit at our out-patient department the diagnosis of subaffective dysthymia, possibly sub-bipolar type, was made. She responded well to imipramine (200 mg/day), and after four weeks she showed a definite hypomanic episode. Imipramine was discontinued, and lithium was given. After two weeks Ms B became severely depressed. Her hypersomnic/retarded, by this time bipolar II, depression was treated in our in-patient department with a non-selective monoamine oxidase inhibitor (nialemide, 150 mg/day) and lithium. After three weeks she was symptom free again, and at six-month follow-up she was taking lithium only, and she wanted to continue her studies at the university.

This is a typical case of subaffective dysthymia, sub-bipolar type, that developed bipolar II depression after the pharmacologically mobilised hypomania. It also demonstrates the importance of family history, and the indicative role of polyglottism in clinical diagnosis in such cases.

Case 3

Mrs C is a 34-year-old married woman. Her father was an aggressive person with severe alcoholism. The mother of Mrs C was an alcoholic too. The patient described her childhood as "absolutely unhappy", and "it would be better to forget it". From age 7 to 17 she suffered from endocarditis, polyarthritis, and nephrolithiasis, and she had pre-menstrual tension from age 17. Mrs C married at age 19. Five years later she divorced, and married again. Her personality was predominantly unstable, with covert aggressive features and antisocial tendencies. During the past 15 years she has had nine jobs, and has abused alcohol in the last seven years. She was referred to our in-patient unit because

> of her suicidal tendencies, which was a consequence of her interpersonal conflict. At admission she was irritable, dysphoric, insomnic, and blaming others. After two weeks of abstinence her condition did not change while taking sedatives. Amitriptyline (75 mg/day) was introduced, but after seven days the drug was discontinued because of anticholinergic side-effects. Her symptoms improved partially on low-dose haloperidol (6 mg/day), administered simultaneously with insight-orientated psychotherapy. Her discharge diagnosis was sociopathy and alcohol abuse. Six months after her discharge she was working, but her complaints persisted.

This is a case of character spectrum depression and demonstrates the significant role of early development in characterologically based persistent dysphoria.

Summary

Our clinical observations and related research findings suggest that the new concept of dysthymic disorder is useful in everyday psychiatric practice. It helps clinicians to improve their diagnostic ability, reducing treatment failures. This concept also suggests that psychiatrists must give up the traditional stereotype in their diagnostic thinking, that is, that 'mild' symptoms automatically indicate neurotic or personality disturbances. The clinical diagnosis has to be based on a special constellation of familial/genetic, developmental, phenomenological, and biological data, rather than on the illness severity alone.

Symposium discussion

DR KATONA: It seemed to me that Dr Rihmer's splendid talk went a long way to answer some of the questions raised by Professor Goldberg about the appropriateness of treatment in relatively mild depressive illnesses.

There was one thing that I think can be found within the evidence you presented and which I am not quite clear on. Although the two groups of dysthymic disorders that you were able to subdivide, the subaffective and the characterological, were similar in severity as measured by the Hamilton scale, they obviously differed very much both in terms of biological measures and in terms of treatment response. What I wondered is whether the relatively mildly ill within the subaffective dysthymia group did as well with treatment as the relatively severe within the subaffective dysthymia group.

DR RIHMER: Thank you for your question. I have shown that the subaffective dysthymics and character spectrum depressives showed the same severity of illness on the Hamilton scale in all previously published studies. In current studies, however, is the severity of the two different subtypes according to the Hamilton scale still being analysed? We do not have any statistical data. According to my clinical practice, I can tell you that both subgroups generally do not differ in severity. I think it is very important to have a guide for diagnosis from a family history or from biological markers or from the developmental history, and so on.

PROFESSOR AKISKAL: Dr Rihmer's excellent paper would perhaps explain why we are having tensions in this meeting. Originally the American concept of affective disorder was quite restricted compared to the British. Now we have a much broader concept that is engulfing what is called neurosis and personality disorders in the UK. In this conference, there were eloquent protests against this, especially Professor Goldberg's, but it would seem to me that the usefulness of the dysthymia concept ultimately has to be tested in the type of studies that Dr Rihmer has presented to us. The real test of a diagnostic system is that it predicts response to a given intervention, or it does not. It remains to be seen whether dysthymic disorder will survive as an entity, but for now it appears to have some usefulness, at least in the hands of many North American practitioners who have found in dysthymia, conceived as a subaffective disorder, the justification to explore treatments that had worked with mood disorders. That is quite gratifying, because ultimately all our efforts are for the benefit of the patient. Thus, nosology should not be viewed as a sterile exercise in statistics; it is ultimately a guide to help the patients and the disabilities that they experience as a result of their disorders, no matter what the labels are.

References

ABRAMS, R. & TAYLOR, M. A. (1976) Catatonia: a prospective clinical study. *Archives of General Psychiatry*, **33**, 579–581.

AKISKAL, H. S. (1981) Subaffective disorders: dysthymic, cyclothymic and bipolar II disorders in the "borderline" realm. *Psychiatric Clinics of North America*, **4**, 25–46.

—— (1982) Factors associated with incomplete recovery in primary depressive illness. *Journal of Clinical Psychiatry*, **43**, 266–271.

—— (1983) Dysthymic disorder: psychopathology of proposed chronic depressive subtypes. *American Journal of Psychiatry*, **140**, 11–20.

——, DJENDEREDJIAN, A. H., ROSENTHAL, R. H., *et al* (1977) Cyclothymic disorder: validating criteria for inclusion in the bipolar affective group. *American Journal of Psychiatry*, **134**, 1227–1233.

——, BITAR, A. H., PUZANTIAN, V. R., *et al* (1978) The nosological status of neurotic depression. *Archives of General Psychiatry*, **35**, 756–766.

——, ROSENTHAL, T. L., HAYKAL, R. F., *et al* (1980) Characterological depressions. Clinical and sleep EEG findings separating "subaffective dysthymias" from "character-spectrum disorders". *Archives of General Psychiatry*, **37**, 777–783.

——, KING, D., ROSENTHAL, T. L., *et al* (1981) Chronic depressions. Part 1. Clinical and familial characteristics in 137 probands. *Journal of Affective Disorders*, **3**, 297–315.

——, CHEN, S. E., DAVIS, G. C., *et al* (1985*a*) Borderline: an adjective in search of a noun. *Journal of Clinical Psychiatry*, **46**, 41–48.

——, YEREVANIAN, B. I., DAVIS, G. C., *et al* (1985*b*) The nosologic status of borderline personality: clinical and polysomnographic study. *American Journal of Psychiatry*, **142**, 192–198.

AMBELAS, A. (1987) Life events and mania. *British Journal of Psychiatry*, **150**, 235–240.

AMERICAN PSYCHIATRIC ASSOCIATION (1980) *Diagnostic and Statistical Manual of Mental Disorders* (3rd edn) (DSM–III). Washington, DC: APA.

ANDREASEN, N. C. (1982) Affective disorders: concept, classification, and diagnosis. In *Handbook of Affective Disorders* (ed. E. S. Paykel), pp. 24–44. New York: The Guildford Press.

BAXTER, L., EDELL, W., GERNER, R., *et al* (1984) Dexamethazone suppression test and axis I diagnosis of inpatients with DSM–III borderline personality disorder. *Journal of Clinical Psychiatry*, **45**, 150–153.

BLAZER, D., GEORGE, L. K., LANDERMAN, R., *et al* (1985) Psychiatric disorders. A rural/urban comparison. *Archives of General Psychiatry*, **42**, 651–656.

BRONISCH, T., WITTCHEN, H-U., KRIEG, C., *et al* (1985) Depressive neurosis. A long-term prospective and retrospective follow-up study of former inpatients. *Acta Psychiatrica Scandinavica*, **71**, 237–248.

DAVIDSON, J. R. T., MILLER, R. D., TURNBULL, C. D., *et al* (1982) Atypical depression. *Archives of General Psychiatry*, **39**, 527–534.

——, KRISHAN, R., FRANCE, R., *et al* (1985) Neurovegetative symptoms in chronic pain and depression. *Journal of Affective Disorders*, **9**, 213–218.

DEPUE, R. A., SLATER, J. F., WOLFSTETTER-KAUSCH, H., *et al* (1981) A behavioural paradigm for identifying persons at risk for bipolar depressive disorder: a conceptual framework and five validation studies. *Journal of Abnormal Psychology*, **90**, 381–437.

EASTWOOD, M. R. & STIASNY, S. (1978) Psychiatric disorder, hospital admission, and season. *Archives of General Psychiatry*, **35**, 769–771.

FIEVE, R. R. & DUNNER, D. L. (1975) Unipolar and bipolar affective states. In *The Nature and Treatment of Depression* (eds F. F. Flach & S. C. Draghi), pp. 145–160. New York: John Wiley and Sons.

HIRSCHFELD, R. M. A. & KLERMAN, G. L. (1979) Personality attributes and affective disorders. *American Journal of Psychiatry*, **136**, 67–70.

KELLER, M. B., LAVORI, P. W., ENDICOTT, J., *et al* (1983) "Double depression": two-year follow-up. *American Journal of Psychiatry*, **140**, 689–694.

KENDELL, R. E. (1985) The diagnosis of mania. *Journal of Affective Disorders*, **8**, 207–213.

KIELHOLZ, P. (1973) *Masked Depression*. Bern: Hans Huber.

LIEBOWITZ, M. R., SATALLONE, F., DUNNER, D. L., *et al* (1979) Personality features of patients with primary affective disorder. *Acta Psychiatrica Scandinavica*, **60**, 214–224.

LLOYD, C. (1980) Life events and depressive disorder reviewed. Part II. Events as precipitating factors. *Archives of General Psychiatry*, **37**, 541–548.

MCNAMARA, M. E., REYNOLDS, C. F., SOLOFF, F. H., *et al* (1984) EEG sleep evaluation of depression in borderline patients. *American Journal of Psychiatry*, **141**, 182–186.

PASKIND, H. A. (1930) Manic-depressive psychoses in private practice. *Archives of Neurology and Psychiatry*, **23**, 787–794.

POPE, H. G. & LIPINSKI, J. F., Jr (1978) Diagnosis in schizophrenia and manic-depressive illness. A reassessment of the specificity of "schizophrenia" symptoms in the light of current research. *Archives of General Psychiatry*, **35**, 811–828.

RIEDER, R. O., MANN, L. S., WEINBERGER, P. R., *et al* (1983) Computed tomographic scans in patients with schizophrenia and bipolar affective disorder. *Archives of General Psychiatry*, **40**, 735–739.

RIHMER, Z. (1982) Polyglottism and depression. *British Journal of Psychiatry*, **140**, 550.

—— & SZUCS, R. (1979) Nem psychotikus depressiok elkulonitese alvasmegvonassal (in Hungarian). *Ideggyogyaszati Szemle*, **32**, 282–284.

——, ARATO, M., SZENTISTVANYI, I., *et al* (1982) The red blood cell/plasma lithium ratio: marker of biological heterogeneity within bipolar affective illness? *Psychiatry Research*, **6**, 197–201.

——, SZADOCZKY, E. & ARATO, M. (1983) Dexamethasone suppression test in masked depression. *Journal of Affective Disorders*, **5**, 293–296.

——, ARATO, M., SZADOCZKY, E., *et al* (1984) The dexamethasone suppression test in psychotic versus non-psychotic endogenous depression. *British Journal of Psychiatry*, **145**, 508–511.

ROY, A., SUTTON, M. & PICKAR, D. (1985) Neuroendocrine and personality variables in dysthymic disorder. *American Journal of Psychiatry*, **142**, 94–97.

SCHATZBERG, A. F. & COLE, J. O. (1978) Benzodiazepines in depressive disorders. *Archives of General Psychiatry*, **35**, 1359–1365.

——, ROTHSCHILD, A. J., STAHL, J. B., *et al* (1983) The dexamethasone suppression test: identification of subtypes of depression. *American Journal of Psychiatry*, **140**, 88–91.

SPITZER, R. L., ENDICOTT, J. & ROBINS, E. (1978) Research diagnostic criteria. Rationale and reliability. *Archives of General Psychiatry*, **35**, 773–782.

STONE, M. H. (1978) Toward early detection of manic-depressive illness in psychoanalytic patients. *American Journal of Psychotherapy*, **32**, 427–439.

SZADOCZKY, E., RIHMER, Z., ARATO, M., *et al* (1983) Adatock az un neurotikus depressziok heterogenitasahoz. A klinikai es neuroendokrinologiai elkulonites lehetosegei (in Hungarian). *Ideggyogyaszati Szemle*, **36**, 461–467.

WATTS, C. A. H. (1957) The mild endogenous depression. *British Medical Journal*, *i*, 4–8.

WEISSMAN, M. M. & KLERMAN, G. L. (1977) The chronic depressive in the community: unrecognized and poorly treated. *Comprehensive Psychiatry*, **18**, 523–532.

—— & MYERS, J. K. (1978) Affective disorders in a US urban community. *Archives of General Psychiatry*, **35**, 1304–1311.

WINOKUR, G., BEHAR, D., VAN VALKENBURG, C., *et al* (1978) Is a familial definition of depression both feasible and valid? *Journal of Nervous and Mental Disease*, **166**, 764–768.

VON KORFF, M., SHAPIRO, S., BURKE, J. D., *et al* (1987) Anxiety and depression in a primary care clinic. *Archives of General Psychiatry*, **44**, 152–156.

Index

Compiled by STANLEY THORLEY